A HANDFUL OF PLEASANT
DELIGHTS

A Handful
of Pleasant Delights
(1584)

By CLEMENT ROBINSON *and*
Divers Others

EDITED BY

HYDER E. ROLLINS

DOVER PUBLICATIONS, INC.
NEW YORK

This Dover edition, first published in 1965, is an unabridged and unaltered republication of the work published by Harvard University Press in 1924.

Library of Congress Catalog Card Number: 65-20488

Manufactured in the United States of America

Dover Publications, Inc.
180 Varick Street
New York 14, N.Y.

INTRODUCTION

THE *Handful of Pleasant Delights*, a miscellany of broadside ballads composed "by Clement Robinson and divers others," is preserved in a unique copy at the British Museum (press-mark C.39.b.46). It came into the possession of the Museum on October 4, 1871, and bears a printed note, clipped from the sale catalogue (1819, p. 164) of the White Knights Library, that runs as follows:

> This is presumed to be the ONLY PERFECT COPY of a very interesting Collection of Old Poetry, which acquires additional interest from the allusion made to the First Poem in the Collection, by the frantic Ophelia when strewing the flowers in her phrenzy: "There's Rosemary, that's for remembrance," &c. See Hamlet, Act IV. Scene V.

The note, however, is inaccurate, for the small quarto volume lacks one leaf (signature B vj). A number of pages, furthermore, are very badly blurred and faded, and others have key-words and signature-marks pared away by the binders. Several pages are almost undecipherable.

Because of Shakespeare's familiarity with it,[1] the *Handful of Pleasant Delights* has long interested scholars. While the single known copy was owned by John Brand and Colonel Byng, several students were permitted to examine it. Joseph Ritson [2] had seen it before 1802;

---

[1] See below, Notes *passim;* and Anders, *Shakespeare's Books,* pp. 166, 169, 173 f., 181, 191, 269.   [2] *Bibliographia Poetica,* p. 311.

George Ellis reprinted two ballads[1] from it in his *Speci-
mens of the Early English Poets* (1803) and Sir Egerton
Brydges two[2] in *Censura Literaria* (1808); Thomas Evans
included several others[3] in his edition of *Old Ballads,
Historical and Narrative* (1810); while, at about the same
time, Edmond Malone, the well-known Shakespearean
scholar, copied the entire book. His transcript remains in
Bodley's Library. In 1815 Thomas Park copied the
Handful and edited it in the second volume of his *Heli-
conia.*[4] At that time the little book had changed owners
at a price that for those days was remarkably high. It
brought £26 5s. at the Brand sale in 1807. The Marquis
of Blandford (later the fifth Duke of Marlborough) was
the purchaser. When his books (the White Knights
Library) were sold in 1819, the *Handful* passed to the
Perry library for £26 15s. 6d.; thence to the Jolley li-
brary in 1822 for £15; and finally, in 1844, to its last
private owner, Thomas Corser, for £25 10s.[5] Edward
Arber records that, when he asked Corser for permission
to reprint the miscellany in his *English Scholar's Library*,
that gentleman refused, "not being in favour of making
English Literature 'as cheap as sixpenny chap-books.'"
The British Museum, of course, was more liberal. In
1871 the book was issued in facsimile for the Spenser

---

[1] Nos. 7 and 17. (The ballads are numbered in the Table of
Contents and in the Notes.)
[2] Nos. 17 and 20.   [3] Nos. 1, 3, 14, 25, 32.
[4] *Heliconia, comprising a Selection of English Poetry of the Eliza-
bethan Age*, 3 vols., London, 1815.
[5] Lowndes, *Bibliographer's Manual*, and Hazlitt, *Handbook to
the Popular . . . Literature of Great Britain*, 1867, *s.v.* Robinson,
Clement.

Society with an introduction by James Crossley.[1] Edward
Arber's edition [2] followed in 1878.

None of these editions are wholly satisfactory. Thomas
Park's text, to use Crossley's words, "was taken from a
very inaccurate transcript of the original unique copy,
and without, as it appears, any collation being made with
the printed book as the sheets passed through the press.
The reproduction therefore . . . may be said to be
nearly worthless. Whole lines are omitted; misprints,
with some times editorial notes upon them as if they were
the actual text, occur in almost every other page; and the
punctuation neither represents that of the original work
nor of any intelligible system." This comment is not too
severe. But, inaccurate as Park's reprint was, for almost
sixty years it alone enabled scholars to know what the
Handful actually contained, so that it served a very use-
ful purpose. At the present time it is extremely difficult
to find, and when found is entirely too expensive for its
real value. James Crossley's edition was rather an at-
tempt at a type-facsimile than an edition. It is not alto-
gether successful in that attempt, and it adds nothing
whatever to Park's notes. The volume, however, is at-
tractively printed, and it enables the reader to picture
the physical appearance of the *Handful*. Arber's edition
of 1878, like the other work of that genial and prolific
scholar, is fairly reliable, and some of his notes are valu-

---

[1] *A Handefull of Pleasant Delites By Clement Robinson and Divers
Others Reprinted from the Original Edition of 1584.* Printed for the
Spenser Society, 1871.

[2] *The English Scholar's Library of Old and Modern Works*, No. 3.
Clement Robinson and divers others. *A Handful of Pleasant De-
lights*, etc., Edited by Edward Arber, London, 1878.

able. But Arber normalized the stanza forms, expanded contractions, and otherwise modernized the original, so that except for the most general purposes his text cannot be trusted.

To-day none of the three editions can be obtained without a prolonged search of the old bookstores. Even then one must be prepared to buy complete sets of *Heliconia*, the *English Scholar's Library*, and the Spenser Society publications, rather than the single volumes of the *Handful*. The three editions are not only practically unobtainable, but furthermore none treats the miscellany from the point of view of balladry, none has a wholly accurate text, and none has a discussion of the problem that gives vital interest to the book — the problem of its date. The need for a new edition is too obvious to require further comment.

The *Handful of Pleasant Delights* contains nothing but ballads, all of which had, before their collection in that miscellany, been printed on broadsides, so that it is a bit surprising to see how unanimous is the praise given to it. As a rule, critics regard broadside ballads as beneath contempt. Thomas Park thought the *Delights* far superior to the poems in *A Gorgeous Gallery of Gallant Inventions* (1578), "being written in general with a modernised tone of versification, which must render them more pleasing to modern readers. Some few indeed may aspire to be praised for higher merit than mere smoothness of verse: particularly . . . [No. 17, line 1214, below], which claims commendation for apposite metaphor, sarcastic sportiveness, ingenious illustration, and moral inference." Crossley called the *Handful* "one of the most prized of

the poetical book gems of the Elizabethan period." Mr.
Charles Crawford[1] considers it "a work of considerable
merit, containing some notable songs"; Sir Sidney Lee[2]
speaks of it as a collection of "lyric poems of varied
length"; and Mr. Harold H. Child[3] comments on the
fact, as if it were extraordinary, that "every poem in the
Handefull has its tune assigned it by name." None of
these gentlemen seem to have recognized that the poems
in the *Handful* are broadside ballads, pure and simple.
As such they were collected by a ballad-writer and pub-
lished by a ballad-printer for the delectation, not of the
literary reader, but of the vulgar, who loved "a ballad in
print a life." The work of Richard Jones, a decidedly
minor printer, ranges in date from 1564 to 1602. He
devoted himself particularly to ballad-printing, and in
the *Handful* he included only a few — perhaps what
seemed to him the best — of his ballads. The *Handful*,
therefore, in its aims affords the greatest possible con-
trast to the miscellanies from *Tottel's* to *A Poetical Rhap-
sody*, which were compiled for an altogether different
group of readers.[4] Many of the ballads in the *Handful*
are pleasing, but it would be an easy matter to pick out
Elizabethan broadside ballads that equal or surpass them

[1] *Englands Parnassus*, Oxford, 1913, p. xix.
[2] *Cambridge History of English Literature*, III, 283.
[3] *Ibid.*, p. 214. Five poems, by the way, have no tunes.
[4] But a few genuine ballads appear in both the *Paradise* and the
Gallery, while several more or less professional ballad-writers —
among them, Thomas Churchyard, John Heywood, William Gray,
and John Canand — contributed ballads (minus tunes) to *Tottel's*.
Many poems from *Tottel's* were reprinted in broadside-ballad form
by Elizabethan printers.

as poetry. Nevertheless, the poetry of the *Handful* is not, on the whole, inferior to that of the *Paradise of Dainty Devises* (1576) or of the *Gorgeous Gallery of Gallant Inventions* (1578).

In 1566 the following entry was made in the Stationers' Register: [1]

> R Jonnes   Recevyd of Rychard Jonnes for his lycense for prynting of a boke intituled of *very pleasaunte Sonettes and storyes in myter* by clament Robynson. . . . . [no sum stated]

It has been generally assumed that the extant edition of the *Handful* is a reissue, with additions, of the *Pleasant Sonnets* of 1566. This was suggested by Ritson.[2] Collier[3] thought that the identity of the two works was not wholly probable, but succeeded in showing that one or two of the ballads that appear in the *Handful* were licensed for publication before the *Pleasant Sonnets*. More recently, most scholars interested in the matter have come to think that the *Pleasant Sonnets* was a first edition of the *Handful*, — among them, W. C. Hazlitt,[4] William Chappell,[5] Sir Sidney Lee,[6] J. W. Ebsworth, and Edward Arber. Ebsworth found in the Bagford Collection in the

---

[1] Arber's *Transcript*, I, 313. Other entries of the *Handful* were made on July 3, 1601; December 13, 1620; August 4, 1626; April 29, 1634; and April 4, 1655. A book called *The parlour of Plesaunte Delightes*, which may have influenced the name of the *Handful*, was licensed on January 13, 1581.

[2] *Bibliographia Poetica*, p. 311.

[3] *Extracts from the Stationers' Registers*, I, 144.

[4] *Handbook*, 1867, p. 515.

[5] *Popular Music of the Olden Time*, I, 91.

[6] *Dictionary of National Biography*, s.v. Robinson, Clement.

British Museum a single leaf [1] which he believed to belong to "an earlier edition" than the *Handful*. Arber did not feel sure that this leaf belonged to an earlier edition, but he attempted — not very successfully [2] — to name the *Handful* ballads that could not have appeared in the *Pleasant Sonnets* of 1566.

Still more recently, critical opinion seems to have undergone a change. Thus Messrs. Seccombe and Allen, in *The Age of Shakespeare* (1903, I, 56), declare positively, but altogether incorrectly, that "in 1584 appeared *A Handefull of Pleasant Delites*, a collection of, up to that time, unpublished lyrics." Mr. Harold H. Child, in the *Cambridge History of English Literature* (1911, III, 212, 214), remarks that the earliest poetical miscellany to follow *Tottel's* was the *Paradise of Dainty Devises* (1576), and adds somewhat doubtfully the statement that the *Handful* "has been thought to be a later edition of the book of 1566." In his edition (1913) of *Englands Parnassus*, Mr. Charles Crawford has expressed this opinion of the matter: "Parts of the work [the *Handful*] must surely have been composed after *A Gorgious Gallery* [1578], for I notice that three poems in it are made up principally from two poems that appear in its predecessor, whole stanzas in each, and several of them coming together in the same order, being worded almost exactly alike. . . . the theory that *A Handefull of Pleasant De-*

---

[1] Reprinted on pp. 73 ff., below.

[2] As I have shown in my article on "The Date, Authors, and Contents of *A Handfull of Pleasant Delights*" (*Journal of English and Germanic Philology*, XVIII, 1919, 43–59), from which much of the material for the Introduction and Notes in this volume has been taken.

lights may be identical with 'A boke of very pleasaunte sonnettes and storyes in myter,' by Clement Robinson, licensed to R. Jhones in 1566, can hardly be entertained when one finds that it is in parts but a rehash of pieces in *A Gorgious Gallery;* but it is possible that Robinson gave a place in his anthology to poems that were previously printed in his book of sonnets and stories." Mr. Crawford gives no references, but the "rehashing" is much more extensive than he suspected. That this rehashing was done by the authors of the poems in the *Gorgeous Gallery*, not by Clement Robinson and his associates, my notes on Nos. 4, 6, 18, 19, 23, and 27 conclusively prove. It follows, naturally enough, that these ballads must have been accessible to the compiler of the *Gorgeous Gallery* before 1578.[1]

There is every reason to believe that the *Handful* was actually issued in 1566. The absence of a license-fee is not unprecedented,[2] and the difference in title between the 1566 entry and the 1584 edition is of no importance. The *Gorgeous Gallery* itself was registered under two other names before its present title was decided on;[3] and it should be observed that the running title of both the *Handful* and the single leaf discovered by Ebsworth is "Sonets and Histories, to sundrie new Tunes," a title much more appropriate for the 1566 entry than for the *Handful* itself. This single leaf [4] beyond all doubt be-

---

[1] Really before 1577, for the *Gallery* was registered at Stationers' Hall on June 5 of that year.

[2] See the Register for the year 1588, when no license-fees are recorded for about half of the entries.

[3] Arber's *Transcript*, II, 313.   [4] See pp. 73 ff., below.

longed to a different edition: it has the page signature
D 2, and bears the last three stanzas of No. 22, all of No.
23, and the first twelve lines of No. 24 (or lines 1581–
1645 in my reprint), and thus corresponds exactly (save
that it has one additional line) to sig. D 4 and *verso* of the
Handful. The edition to which it belonged, then, pre-
sumably had two signatures, or four pages, fewer than
the *Handful*; and, as three or four of the ballads printed
in the latter before sig. D 4 can be proved to have been
written during the years 1572–1582, it seems probable
that this leaf was part of an edition earlier than that of
1584 — an edition representing the *Pleasant Sonnets* of
the entry in 1566. This probability is made almost a
certainty by the typography of the leaf: the type
clearly indicates a date earlier than 1584.

The title-page of the *Handful*, it may be superfluous
to add, in itself offers proof that there had been an earlier
edition. It announces that the book contains "sundrie
new Sonets. . . . *Newly* deuised to the *newest* tunes. . . .
With *new additions* of certain Songs, to *verie late* deuised
Notes, not commonly knowen, nor *vsed heretofore*." But
this is false from beginning to end. Like the typical
dishonest stationer whose "character" George Wither
was later to portray so vividly, Richard Jones provided
this new title-page to delude customers into buying old
wares. Most of the ballads had been printed before 1566,
and the tunes were so old and are now so hard to trace that
even William Chappell, an authority whose knowledge
of popular tunes was unrivalled, could include only four
or five of them in his *Popular Music of the Olden Time*.
The fact that tunes are nearly always named for the bal-

lads in the *Handful* entitles that miscellany to the credit
of being the first of the "garlands" — frank collections
of broadside ballads — which in the hands of Thomas
Deloney, Richard Johnson, and Martin Parker became,
in later years, extremely popular.

Of Clement Robinson, whose name appears on the
title-page of the *Handful*, little is known. It is obvious,
however, that he was at the height of his ballad-writing
in 1566, when his name was given in the Stationers' Reg-
ister as the compiler of the *Pleasant Sonnets*. W. C.
Hazlitt [1] conjectured, not unreasonably, that he was the
C. R. whose initials are signed to a prose broadside on
a "marueilous straunge Fishe" [2] that was printed in
1569; and Mr. Collmann [3] has plausibly suggested that
he was the Robinson who in 1566 entered into a ballad-
flyting with Thomas Churchyard. The very fact that
Robinson's name occurs on the title-page of the 1584
edition strengthens the presumption that the book was a
reissue of the *Pleasant Sonnets* that had been registered
eighteen years earlier.

The dates of the individual ballads are, with a few
exceptions, established in the Notes (pp. 80 ff., below),
which prove that most of the ballads in the *Handful* had
been printed before the registration of the *Pleasant Son-
nets* in 1566. To summarize the data there given: Nos.
3, 7, 14, and 29 were certainly not in the 1566 edition;
probably Nos. 1 and 15 were not; and there is no evi-
dence to show whether Nos. 21, 26, 28, and 31 were in

---

[1] *Handbook*, 1867, p. 515.
[2] Reprinted in Lilly's *79 Black-Letter Ballads*, p. 145.
[3] *Ballads and Broadsides*, 1912, pp. 81–82.

print by 1566 or were added to the 1584 *Handful.* The remaining ballads — twenty-two in all — could have been, and most probably were, in the manuscript of the *Pleasant Sonnets* which the Stationers' clerk registered in 1566; and that this manuscript was actually printed the same year hardly admits of doubt.

With the date of 1566 established for the first edition of the *Handful,* the book immediately assumes a much more important rank in the history of Elizabethan literature than that heretofore granted it. Suggested, no doubt, by the success of *Tottel's,* — which had reached a fourth edition in 1565, — the *Handful,* following in 1566, became the second, and not the fourth, poetical miscellany, preceding instead of succeeding the *Paradise of Dainty Devises* and the *Gorgeous Gallery of Gallant Inventions.* On both of those miscellanies it exerted considerable influence. That it was popular among Elizabethan readers in general the Notes will show.

In the present edition the texts are reprinted line for line, page for page. The original punctuation is retained throughout and, since it never really obscures the meaning, is not corrected or commented on in the Notes. Key-words and signature-marks that have been cut off, and letters that were dropped from the form in printing, leaving vacant spaces, have been supplied between square brackets; and obvious misprints (like inverted letters) are corrected in the text. All such bracketed and corrected words, however, are enumerated in the "List of Misprints and Variant Readings," where, too, a collation of the texts of the three modern editions is given.

In this reprint the typography of the title-page is followed exactly, — except that long ſ is everywhere printed as s, — but the black letter of the text is represented below by roman type and roman type by italics. The numbering of lines and pages is, of course, an editorial addition.

Grateful acknowledgment is made to the officials of the British Museum for permission to reprint the unique text of the *Handful;* to my master, Professor George Lyman Kittredge, for many helpful suggestions about the Glossary and the Notes; and to my friend, Miss Addie F. Rowe, for invaluable assistance in the proofreading.

H. E. R.

NEW YORK CITY, April 21, 1923.

CONTENTS

A Handefull

of pleasant delites,

Containing sundrie new Sonets
and delectable Histories, in
diuers kindes of Meeter.

Newly deuised to the newest tunes
that are now in vse, to be sung:
euerie Sonet orderly pointed
to his proper Tune.

With new additions of certain Songs,
to verie late deuised Notes, not
commonly knowen, nor
vsed heretofore,

By Clement Robinson,
and diuers others.

¶AT LONDON

Printed by Richard Ihones : dwel-
ling at the signe of the Rose
and Crowne, neare
Holburne Bridge
1 5 8 4.

The Printer to

the Reader.

YOu that in Musicke do delight
    your minds for to solace:
This little booke of Sonets m[ight]   5
    wel like you in that case,
Peruse it wel ere you passe by,
    here may you wish and haue,
Such pleasant songs to ech new tune,
    as lightly you can craue.   10
Or if fine Histories you would reade,
    you need not far to seek:
Within this booke such may you haue,
    as Ladies may wel like.
Here may you haue such pretie thinges,   15
    as women much desire:
Here may you haue of sundrie sorts,
    such Songs as you require.
Wherefore my friend, if you regard,
    such Songs to reade or heare: 20
Doubt not to buy this pretie Booke,
    the price is not so deare.

                Farewell.

A Nosegaie alwaies

sweet, for Louers to send for Tokens,
of loue, at Newyeres tide, or for fairings,
as they in their minds shall be disposed to write.

A Nosegaie lacking flowers fresh,   5
    to you now I do send.
Desiring you to look thereon,
    when that you may intend:
For flowers fresh begin to fade,
    and *Boreas* in the field,   10
Euen with his hard coniealed frost,
    no better flowers doth yeeld:
¶ But if that winter could haue sprung,
    a sweeter flower than this,
I would haue sent it presently   15
    to you withouten misse:
Accept this then as time doth serue,
    be thankful for the same,
Despise it not, but keep it well,
    and marke ech flower his name.   20
¶ *Lauander* is for louers true,
    which euermore be faine:
Desiring alwaies for to haue,
    some pleasure for their pain:
And when that they obtained haue,   25
    the loue that they require,
Then haue they al their perfect ioie,
    and quenched is the fire.

¶ *Rosemarie* is for remembrance,   31
    betweene vs daie and night:
Wishing that I might alwaies haue,
    you present in my sight.
And when I cannot haue,   35
    as I haue said before,
Then *Cupid* with his deadly dart,
    doth wound my heart full sore.
¶ *Sage* is for sustenance,
    that should mans life sustaine,   40
For I do stil lie languishing,
    continually in paine,
And shall do stil vntil I die,
    except thou fauour show:
My paine and all my greeuous smart,   45
    ful wel you do it know.
¶ *Fenel* is for flaterers,
    an euil thing it is sure:
But I haue alwaies meant truely,
    with constant heart most pure: 50
And will continue in the same,
    as long as life doth last,
Still hoping for a ioiful daie,
    when all our paines be past.
¶ *Violet* is for faithfulnesse,   55
    which in me shall abide:
Hoping likewise that from your heart,
    you wil not let it slide.
And wil continue in the same,
    as you haue nowe begunne: 60
                 And

And then for euer to abide,
   then you my heart haue wonne.
¶ *Time* is to trie me,   65
   as ech be tried must,
[Le]tting you know while life doth last,
   I wil not be vniust,
And if I should I would to God,
   to hell my soule should beare.   70
And eke also that *Belzebub*,
   with teeth he should me teare.
¶ *Roses* is to rule me.
   with reason as you will,
For to be still obedient,   75
   your minde for to fulfill:
And thereto will not disagree,
   in nothing that you say:
But will content your mind truely,
   in all things that I may.   80
¶ *Ieliflowers* is for gentlenesse,
   which in me shall remaine:
Hoping that no sedition shal,
   depart our hearts in twaine.
As soone the sunne shal loose his course,   85
   the moone against her kinde,
Shall haue no light, if that I do
   once put you from my minde.
¶ *Carnations* is for gratiousnesse,
   marke that now by the way,   90
Haue no regard to flatterers,
   nor passe not what they say.
               A iii   For

For they will come with lying tales,   95
    your eares for to fulfil:
In anie case do you consent,
    nothing vnto their wil.
¶ *Marigolds* is for marriage,
    that would our minds suffise,   100
Least that suspition of vs twaine,
    by anie meanes should rise:
As for my part, I do not care,
    my self I wil stil vse,
That all the women in the world,   105
    for you I will refuse.
¶ *Peniriall* is to print your loue,
    so deep within my heart:
That when you look this Nosegay on,
    my pain you may impart,   110
And when that you haue read the same,
    consider wel my wo,
Think ye then how to recompence,
    euen him that loues you so.
¶ *Cowsloppes* is for counsell,   115
    for secrets vs between,
That none but you and I alone,
    should know the thing we meane:
And if you wil thus wisely do,
    as I think to be best: 120
Then haue you surely won the field,
    and set my heart at rest.
I pray you keep this Nosegay wel,
    and set by it some store:
                 And   125

And thus farewel, the Gods thee guide,
    both now and euermore.
Not as the common sort do vse,
    to set it in your brest: 130
That when the smel is gone away,
    on ground he takes his rest.

FINIS.

L. Gibsons Tantara, wherin Danea wel-
commeth home her Lord Diophon frō the war. 135
To the tune of, Down right Squire.

YOu Lordings, cast off your weedes of
    me thinks I heare   (wo
    A trūpet shril which plain doth show
      my Lord is neare: 140
Tantara tara tantara,
    this trumpet glads our hearts,
Therefore to welcome home your King,
    you Lordings plaie your parts,
      Tantara tara tantara, &c.   145
¶ Harke harke, me thinkes I heare again,
    this trumpets voice,
He is at hand this is certaine,
    wherefore reioice.
Tantara tara tantara, &c.   150
    this trumpet still doth say,
With trumpets blast, all dangers past,
    doth shew in Marshall ray.
A iiii   ¶A

¶ A ioifull sight my hearts delight,   156
    my *Diophon* deere:
Thy comely grace, I do embrace,
    with ioiful cheere:
Tantara tara tantara,   160
    what pleasant sound is this,
Which brought to me with victorie,
    my ioy and onely blisse.
      Tantara tara tantara, &c.
        Diophon.   165
My Queene and wife, my ioy and life
    in whom I minde:
In euery part, the trustiest hart,
    that man can finde.
Tantara tara tantara,   170
    me thinks I heare your praise,
Your vertues race in euerie place,
    which trumpet so doth raise.
      Tantara tara tantara, &c.
¶ Now welcome home to *Siria* soile,   175
    from battered field:
That valiantly thy foes did foile,
    with speare and shield:
Tantara tara tantara,
    me thinks I heare it still,   180
Thy sounding praise, abroad to raise,
    with trump that is most shrill,
      Tantara tara tantara, &c.
¶ If honour and fame, O noble Dame,
    such deeds do aske: 185
            Then

Then *Diophon* here to purchase fame,
   hath done this taske:
Tantara tara tantara,   190
   returnd he is againe,
To leade his life, with thee his wife,
   in ioie without disdaine.
     Tantara tara tantara, &c.
       Finis. L. G.   195

¶ *A proper new Song made by a Studient*
in Cambridge, To the tune of I wish to
see those happie daies.

I Which was once a happie wight,
   and hie in Fortunes grace: 200
 And which did spend my golden prime,
   in running pleasures race,
 Am now enforst of late,
   contrariwise to mourne,
 Since fortune ioies, into annoies,   205
   my former state to turne.
¶ The toiling oxe, the horse, the asse,
   haue time to take their rest,
Yea all things else which Nature wrought,
   sometimes haue ioies in brest: 210
   Saue onelie I and such
     which vexed are with paine:
    For still in teares, my life it weares,
    and so I must remaine.
¶ How oft haue I in folded armes,   215
   enioied my delight,

              How

How oft haue I excuses made,
   of her to haue a sight?   220
      But now to fortunes wil,
         I caused am to bow.
      And for to reape a hugie heape,
         which youthful yeares did sow.
¶ Wherefore all ye which do as yet,   225
   remaine and bide behind:
Whose eies dame beauties blazing beams,
   as yet did neuer blind.
      Example let me be,
         to you and other more: 230
      Whose heauie hart, hath felt the smart,
         subdued by *Cupids* lore.
¶ Take heed of gazing ouer much,
   on Damsels faire vnknowne:
For oftentimes the Snake doth lie,   235
   with roses ouergrowde:
      And vnder fairest flowers,
         do noisome Adders lurke:
      Of whom take heed, I thee areed:
         least that thy cares they worke.   240
¶ What though that she doth smile on thee,
   perchance shee doth not loue:
And though she smack thee once or twice,
   she thinks thee so to prooue,
      And when that thou dost thinke,   245
         she loueth none but thee:
      She hath in store, perhaps some more,
         which so deceiued be,
                  Trust

¶ Trust not therefore the outward shew   251
    beware in anie case:
For good conditions do not lie,
    where is a pleasant face:
      But if it be thy chaunce,   255
        a louer true to haue:
      Be sure of this, thou shalt not misse,
        ech thing that thou wilt craue.
¶ And when as thou (good Reader) shalt
    peruse this scrole of mine: 260
Let this a warning be to thee,
    and saie a friend of thine,
      Did write thee this of loue,
        and of a zealous mind:
      Because that he sufficiently,   265
        hath tried the female kind.
¶ Here *Cambridge* now I bid farewell,
    adue to Students all:
Adue vnto the Colledges,
    and vnto *Gunuil* Hall: 270
      And you my fellowes once,
        pray vnto *Ioue* that I
      May haue releef, for this my grief,
        and speedie remedie.
¶ And that he shield you euerichone,   275
    from Beauties luring looks:
Whose baite hath brought me to my baine,
    and caught me from my Books:
      Wherefore, for you, my praier shall be,
        to send you better grace,   280
               That

That modestie with honestie,
   may guide your youthfull race.
Finis quod Thomas Richardson, sometime   285
   Student in Cambridge.

¶ *The scoffe of a Ladie, as pretie as may be,*
   to a yong man that went a wooing:
He wēt stil about her, & yet he wēt without
   because he was so long a dooing.   (*her,* 290

A Ttend thee, go play thee,
   Sweet loue I am busie:
     my silk and twist is not yet spun:
   My Ladie will blame me,
If that she send for me,   295
   and find my worke to be vndun:
     How then?
How shall I be set me?
To say loue did let me?
   Fie no, it will not fit me,   300
   It were no scuse for me.
¶ If loue were attained,
My ioies were vnfained,
   my seame and silke wil take no hold:
Oft haue I beene warned,   305
By others proofe learned:
   hote wanton loue soone waxeth cold,
     Go now:
I say go pack thee,
Or my needle shal prick thee: 310
       Go

Go seeke out Dame Idle:
More fit for thy bridle,
More fit for thy bridle.   315
¶ Wel worthie of blaming,
For thy long detaining,
    all vaine it is that thou hast done:
Best now to be wandring,
Go vaunt of thy winning,   320
    and tell thy Dame what thou hast won:
      Say this:
Then say as I bade thee:
That the little dogge Fancie,
Lies chaste without moouing,   325
    And needeth no threatning,
    For feare of wel beating.
    For feare of wel beating.
¶ The boy is gone lurking,
Good Ladies be working,   330
    dispatch a while that we had done,
The tide will not tarrie,
All times it doth varie,
    The day doth passe, I see the Sun,
The frost bites faire flowers,   335
Lets worke at due howres,
    Haste, haste, and be merie,
    Till our needles be werie.
    Till our needles be werie,
¶ Now Ladies be merie,   340
Because you are werie:
    leaue worke I say, and get you home,
                Your

Your businesse in slacking,   345
Your louer is packing:
    your answer hath cut off his comb.
       How then?
The fault was in him sir,
He wooed it so trim sir,   350
    Alas poore seelie fellow,
    Make much of thy pillow.
    Make much of thy pillow.   *Finis.*

An answer as pretie to the scof of his Lady,
    by the yongman that came a wooing,   355
      Wherein he doth flout her,
    Being glad he went without her,
      Misliking both her and her dooing.

A Las Loue, why chafe ye?
   Why fret ye, why fume ye?   360
    to me it seemeth verie strange,
    Me thinks ye misuse me,
So soone to refuse me,
    vnlesse you hope of better change:
       Wel, wel: 365
Wel now, I perceiue ye,
You are mindful to leaue me:
    Now sure it doth grieue me:
    That I am vnworthie:
    That I am vnworthie.   370
¶ I mean not to let ye, nor I can not forget
    it wil not so out of my minde: (ye,
My loue is not daintie, I see you haue plenty
    that set so little by your friend.
                   Goe   375

Goe too spin on now I pray you, I list not to
    I will goe play me: (stay,
    I am vnfit for you, &c.
Leaue off to flout now, & prick on your clout   380
    you are a daintie Dame indeed,   (now
And thogh of your taūting, I may make my
   as bad or worse thā I shal speed: (vaunting
Sweet heart, though now you forsake it.
I trust you wil take it: 385
and sure I spak it, as fine as you make it, &c
Now wil I be trudging, without anie. grud-
    I am content to giue you ground: (ging
Good reson doth bind me, to leue you behind
    for you are better lost than found: (me,   390
Go play, go seeke out Dame pleasure:
You are a trim treasure,
    Wise women be daintie,
    Of fooles there be plentie, &c.
¶ If I might aduise ye, few words shuld suf-   395
    & yet you shold bestow them wel: (fice ye
Maids must be manerly, not ful of scurility,
    wherein I see you do excel,
Farewel good *Nicibicetur,*
God send you a sweeter,   400
A lustie lim lifter, you are a trim shifter, &c.
                Finis. Peter Picks.

¶ *Dame Beauties replie to the Louer late at*
   libertie: and now complaineth himselfe
   to be her captiue, Intituled: Where is   405
   the life that late I led.
                    The

THe life that erst thou ledst my friend,
    was pleasant to thine eies: 410
    But now the losse of libertie,
      thou seemest to despise.
Where then thou ioiedst thy will,
    now thou doest grudge in heart:
Then thou no paine nor grief didst feele,   415
    but now thou pinest in smart.
What mooued thee vnto loue,
    expresse and tell the same:
Saue fancie thine, that heapt thy paine,
    thy follie learne to blame.   420
¶ For when thou freedome didst enioie,
    thou gauest thy selfe to ease,
And letst self-will the ruling beare,
    thy fancie fond to please:
Then stealing *Cupid* came,   425
    with bow and golden dart:
He struck the stroke, at pleasure he
    that now doth paine thy hart:
Blame not the Gods of loue,
    But blame thy self thou maist: 430
For freedome was disdaind of thee,
    and bondage more thou waiest.
¶ Who list, thou saist, to liue at rest,
    and freedome to possesse:
The sight of gorgeous Dames must shun,   435
    least loue do them distresse:
Thou blamest *Cupidoes* craft,
    who strikes in stealing sort:

                      And

And sets thee midst the princely Dames,   441
    of Beauties famous fort:
And meaning wel thou saiest,
    as one not bent to loue,
Then *Cupid* he constrains thee yeeld,   445
    as thou thy self canst prooue.
¶ Faire Ladies lookes in libertie,
    enlarged not thy paine:
Ne yet the sight of gorgeous Dames,
    could cause thee thus complaine.   450
It was thy self indeed,
    that causd thy pining woe,
Thy wanton wil, and idle minde,
    causd *Cupid* strike the blow:
Blame not his craft, nor vs   455
    that Beauties darlings be,
Accuse thy selfe to seeke thy care,
    thy fancie did agree.
¶ There is none thou saist, that can
    more truely iudge the case: 460
Than thou that hast the wound receiu'de,
    by sight of Ladies face.
Her beautie thee bewitcht,
    thy minde that erst was free:
Her corps so comely framd, thou saiest,   465
    did force thee to agree:
Thou gauest thy self it seemes,
    her bondman to abide,
Before that her good willingnesse,
    of thee were knowen and tride.   470

What

What iudgement canst thou giue:
   how dost thou plead thy case:
It was not she that did thee wound,   475
   although thou seest her face:
Ne could her beautie so,
   inchaunt or vex thy sprites,
Ne feature hers so comely framde,
   could weaken so thy wits.   480
But that thou mightest haue showne
   the cause to her indeede,
Who spares to speak, thy self dost know,
   doth faile of grace to speede.
¶ By this thou saiest, thou soughtst ẙ means   485
   of torments that you beare,
By this thou wouldest men take heede,
   and learne of loue to feare:
For taking holde thou telst,
   to flie it is too late,   490
And no where canst thou shrowd thy self,
   but Care must be thy mate.
Though loue do pleasure seeme,
   yet plagues none such there are:
Therefore all louers now thou willst,   495
   of liking to beware.
¶ Thy self hath sought the meane and way,
   and none but thou alone:
Of all the grief and care you beare,
   as plainely it is showne: 500
Then why should men take heed,
   thy counsell is vnfit:

                            Thou

Thou sparedst to speak, and faildst to speed, 505
   thy will had banisht wit.
And now thou blamest loue,
   and Ladies faire and free:
And better lost than found my frind,
   your cowards heart we see. *Finis. I.P.* 510

A new Courtly Sonet, of the Lady Green
* sleeues. To the new tune of Greensleeues.*

Greensleeues was all my ioy,
   Greensleeues was my delight:
Greensleeues was my hart of gold, 515
   And who but Ladie Greensleeues.

A Las my loue, ye do me wrong,
   to cast me off discurteously:
And I haue loued you so long,
   Delighting in your companie. 520
  Greensleeues was all my ioy,
   Greensleeues was my delight:
  Greensleeues was my heart of gold,
   And who but Ladie Greensleeues.
¶ I haue been readie at your hand, 525
   to grant what euer you would craue.
I haue both waged life and land,
   your loue and good will for to haue.
   Greensleeues was all my ioy, &c.
¶ I bought thee kerchers to thy head, 530
   that were wrought fine and gallantly:

I kept thee both at boord and bed,
   Which cost my purse wel fauouredly,   535
      Greensleeues was al my ioie, &c.
¶ I bought thee peticotes of the best,
   the cloth so fine as fine might be:
I gaue thee iewels for thy chest,
   and all this cost I spent on thee.   540
      Greensleeues was all my ioie, &c.
¶ Thy smock of silk, both faire and white,
   with gold embrodered gorgeously:
Thy peticote of Sendall right:
   and thus I bought thee gladly.   545
      Greensleeues was all my ioie, &c.
¶ Thy girdle of gold so red,
   with pearles bedecked sumptuously:
The like no other lasses had,
   and yet thou wouldst not loue me,   550
      Greensleeues was all my ioy, &c.
¶ Thy purse and eke thy gay guilt kniues,
   thy pincase gallant to the eie:
No better wore the Burgesse wiues,
   and yet thou wouldst not loue me.   555
      Greensleeues was all my ioy, &c.
¶ Thy crimson stockings all of silk,
   with golde all wrought aboue the knee,
Thy pumps as white as was the milk,
   and yet thou wouldst not loue me.   560
      Greensleeues was all my ioy, &c.
¶ Thy gown was of the grossie green,
   thy sleeues of Satten hanging by:
                Which

Which made thee be our haruest Queen,   566
   and yet thou wouldst not loue me.
      Greensleeues was all my ioy, &c.
¶ Thy garters fringed with the golde,
   And siluer aglets hanging by,   570
Which made thee blithe for to beholde,
   And yet thou wouldst not loue me.
      Greensleeues was all my ioy, &c.
¶ My gayest gelding I thee gaue,
   To ride where euer liked thee,   575
No Ladie euer was so braue,
   And yet thou wouldst not loue me.
      Greensleeues was all my ioy, &c.
¶ My men were clothed all in green,
   And they did euer wait on thee: 580
Al this was gallant to be seen,
   and yet thou wouldst not loue me.
      Greensleeues was all my ioy, &c.
¶ They set thee vp, they took thee downe,
   they serued thee with humilitie,   585
Thy foote might not once touch the ground,
   and yet thou wouldst not loue me.
      Greensleeues was all my ioy, &c.
¶ For euerie morning when thou rose,
   I sent thee dainties orderly: 590
To cheare thy stomack from all woes,
   and yet thou wouldst not loue me.
      Greensleeues was all my ioy, &c.
¶ Thou couldst desire no earthly thing.
   But stil thou hadst it readily: 595
         B iii   [Thy]

Thy musicke still to play and sing,
   And yet thou wouldst not loue me.
      Greensleeues was all my ioy, &c.   600
¶ And who did pay for all this geare,
   that thou didst spend when pleased thee?
Euen I that am reiected here,
   and thou disdainst to loue me.
      Greensleeues was all my ioy, &c.   605
¶ Wel, I wil pray to God on hie,
   that thou my constancie maist see:
And that yet once before I die,
   thou wilt vouchsafe to loue me.
      Greensleeues was all my ioy, &c.   610
¶ Greensleeues now farewel adue,
   God I pray to prosper thee:
For I am stil thy louer true,
   come once againe and loue me.
      Greensleeues was all my ioy, &c.   615
        Finis.

*A proper sonet, wherin the Louer dolefully
sheweth his grief to his L. & requireth pity.
To the tune of, Row wel ye Marriners.*

AS one without refuge,   620
   For life doth pleade with panting
   And rufully the Iudge,   (breath
   Beholds (whose doome grants life or
So fare I now my onelie Loue,   (death,
Whom I tender as Turtle Doue,   625
   Whose tender looks (O ioly ioy)
   Shall win me sure your louing boy:
        [Faire]

Faire lookes, sweet Dame, 630
Or else (alas) I take my bane:
Nice talke, coying,
Wil bring me sure to my ending,
¶ Too little is my skil,
By pen (I saie) my loue to paint, 635
And when that my good will,
My tong wold shew, my heart doth faint:
Sith both the meanes do faile therefore,
My loue for to expresse with lore:
The torments of my inward smart. 640
You may well gesse within your hart:
Wherefore, sweet wench,
Some louing words, this heat to quench
Fine smiles, smirke lookes,
And then I neede no other lookes, 645
¶ Your gleams hath gript the hart,
alas within my captiue breast:
O how I feele the smart,
And how I find my grief increast:
My fancie is so fixt on you, 650
That none away the same can do:
My deer vnlesse you it remooue:
Without redresse I die for loue,
Lament with me,
Ye Muses nine, where euer be, 655
My life I loth,
My Ioies are gone, I tel you troth,
¶ All Musicks solemne found,
Of song, of else of instrument:
B iiii　　　　　Me 660

Me thinks they do resound,
   with doleful tunes, me to lament,
And in my sleep vnsound, alas,
Me thinks such dreadful things to passe: 665
   that out I crie in midst of dreames,
Wherwith my tears run down as streams,
    O Lord, think I,
    She is not here that should be by:
      What chance is this,   670
      That I embrace that froward is?
¶ The Lions noble minde,
   His raging mood (you know) oft staies,
When beasts do yeeld by kinde,
   On them (forsooth) he neuer praies: 675
Then sithence that I am your thrall,
To ease my smart on you I call.
   A bloudie conquest is your part,
   To kill so kind a louing heart:
    Alas remorce,   680
    Or presently I die perforce:
   God grant pitie,
   Within your breast now planted be.
¶ As nature hath you deckt,
   with worthie gifts aboue the rest,   685
So to your praise most great,
   Let pitie dwell within your brest,
That I may saie with heart and wil,
Lo, this is she that might me kil:
   For why? in hand she held the knife,   690
   And yet (forsooth) she saued my life.

                Hey

Hey-ho, darling:
With lustie loue, now let vs sing,   695
Plaie on, Minstrel,
My Ladie is mine onelie girle.

The Historie of Diana and Acteon.
To the Quarter Braules.

D Iana and her darlings deare,   700
Walkt once as you shall heare:
Through woods and waters cleare,
    themselues to play:
The leaues were gay and green,
And pleasant to be seen: 705
They went the trees between,
    in coole aray,
So long, that at the last they found a place,
    of waters full cleare:
So pure and faire a Bath neuer was   710
    found many a yeare.
There shee went faire and gent,
Her to sport, as was her wonted sort:
    In such desirous sort:
    Thus goeth the report: 715
Diana dainteously began her selfe therein to
    And her body for to laue,   (bathe
    So curious and braue.
¶ As they in water stood,
Bathing their liuelie blood: 720
Acteon in the wood,
    chaunst to come by:
And vewed their bodies bare,

                                        [Mar-]

Maruailing what they weare,   726
And stil deuoid of care,
   on them cast his eie:
But when the Nymphs had perceiued him,
   aloud then they cried,   730
Enclosed her, and thought to hide her skin,
   which he had spied:
But too true I tell you,
   She seene was,
    For in height she did passe,   735
    Ech Dame of her race,
    Harke then *Acteons* case:
Whē *Diana* did perceue, where *Acteon* did
   She took bowe in her hand,   (stand,
   And to shoot she began.   740
¶ As she began to shoot, *Acteon* ran about,
To hide he thought no boote,
   his sights were dim:
And as he thought to scape,
Changed was *Acteons* shape,   745
Such was vnluckie fate,
   yeelded to him:
For *Diana* brought it thus to passe,
   and plaied her part,
So that poore *Acteon* changed was   750
   to a hugie Hart,
And did beare, naught but haire:
   In this change,
   Which is as true as strange,
   And thus did he range,   755
           Abroad

[Signature B vj is lacking.]

[Signature B vj is lacking.]

So that his sorrowes importunate,
Had ended his life incontinent,
    Had not Lady *Venus* grace, Lady Lady,   760
    Pitied her poore seruants case,
       My deer Ladie.
¶ For when she saw the torments strong,
Wherewith the Knight was sore opprest,
Which he God knowes had suffered long,   765
Al through this Ladies mercilesse,
    Of their desires she made exchange,
       Ladie, Ladie.
And wrought a myracle most strange,
       My deer Ladie.   770
¶ So that this Ladie faithfully,
Did loue this Knight aboue all other:
And he vnto the contrarie,
Did hate her then aboue all measure,
And pitifull she did complaine: ladie, ladie.   775
Requiring fauour, and might not obtaine.
       My deer ladie.
¶ But when she saw, that in no case,
She might vnto his loue attaine:
And that she could not finde some grace,   780
To ease her long enduring paine,
And ẙ his hart wold not remoue.   Lady, ladie
Without all cure he died for loue,   My deer.
¶ Besides these matters maruelous,
One other thing I wil you tell: 785
Of one whose name was *Narcissus*,
A man whose beautie doth excel.
                 Of

Of natures gifts he had no misse, Lady, lady   790
He had y̆ whole of beauties blisse, My deere.
¶ So that out of manie a far Countrey,
I reade of manie a woman faire,
Did come this *Narcissus* to see,
Who perished when they came there,   795
Through his default I say in fine, lady, lady
Who vnto loue would not incline.   My deer.
¶ Whose disobedience vnto loue,
When vnto *Venus* it did appeare.
How that his hart would not remoue,   800
She punisht him as you shal heare:
    A thing most strange forsooth it was,
        Ladie, Ladie.
Now harken how it came to passe, My deer.
¶ For when he went vpon a daie,   805
With other mo in strange disguise,
Himself forsooth he did aray
    In womans attire of a new deuise,
And ouer a bridge as he did go.   Ladie, ladie.
In the water he sawe his own shadow, My.   810
¶ Which when he did perceiue and see,
A Ladie faire he saith it seemeth:
Forgat himself that it was he,
And iudgde that it was *Dianaes* Nymph,
Who in the waters in such fashion, Lady, la[dy] 815
Did vse themselues for recreation, My deer.
¶ And through the beautie of whose looks,
Taken he was with such fond desire,
That after manie humble sutes,
              Inconti- 820

Incontinent he did aspire.
Vnto her grace him to refer, Ladie, Ladie
Trusting $\overset{t}{y}$ mercie was in her, My deer, &c.
¶ With armes displaid he took his race,   825
And leapt into the riuer there,
And thought his Ladie to imbrace,
Being of himselfe, deuoid of feare,
And there was drownd without redresse,
His crueltie rewarded was,   (Ladie, Ladie.   830
    with such follie.
¶ Loe, hereby you may perceiue,
How *Venus* can, and if she please,
Her disobedient Subiects grieue,
And make them drinke their owne disease,   835
Wherfore rebel not I you wish, Lady, lady.
Least that your chaunce be worse than this,
    if worse may be.   *Finis.*

The Louer cōplaineth the losse of his Ladie
            To Cicilia Pauin.   840

H Eart, what makes thee thus to be,
      in extreame heauinesse?
    If care do cause all thy distresse,
      Why seekest thou not some redresse,
        to ease thy carefulnesse?   845
Hath *Cupid* stroke in Venerie,
Thy wofull corps in ieoperdie:
    right wel then may I sob and crie,   (trie
Til that my Mistresse deer, my faith may
Why would I cloake from her presence,   850
My loue and faithfull diligence?
                            And

And cowardly thus to die.

And cowardly thus to die.   855

¶ No, no, I wil shew my woe,
   in this calamitie.

To her whom Nature shapte so free:

With all *Dianaes* chastitie,
   or *Venus* rare beautie: 860

Then shall I brace felicitie,

And liue in all prosperitie.
   then leaue off this woe, let teares go,
   thou shalt embrace thy Ladie deer ẇ ioy.

In these thy armes so louingly,   865

As *Paris* did faire *Helenie.*
   By force of blinded boy.
   By force of blinded boy.

¶ If *Venus* would grant vnto me,
   such happinesse: 870

As she did vnto *Troylus,*

By help of his friend *Pandarus,*
   To *Cressids* loue who worse,
   Than all the women certainly:
   That euer liued naturally.   875

Whose slight falsed faith, the storie saith,

Did breed by plagues, her great and sore di-
   For she became so leprosie,   (stresse,
   That she did die in penurie:
     Because she did transgresse.   880
     Because she did transgresse.

¶ If she, I saie, wil me regard,
   in this my ieoperdie,

I

l wil shew her fidelitie, 886
And eke declare her curtesie,
　to Louers far and nie:
O heart how happie shouldst thou be,
When my Ladie doth smile on me: 890
　Whose milde merie cheare,
　Wil driue away feare,
Cleane from my brest, and set ioy in ẙ place
　when I shall kisse so tenderly:
Her fingers small and slenderly, 895
　which doth my heart solace, &c.
Therefore ye amorous imps who burne
　so stil in *Cupids* fire,
Let this the force of my retire
Example be to your desire, 900
　That so to loue aspire:
　For I did make deniance,
　And set her at defiance:
　Which made me full wo, it chanced so,
Because I look at my mistresse so coy: 905
Therefore, when she is merily
Disposed, look you curteously:
　Receiue her for your ioy.
　Receiue her for your ioy.
　　　　Finis.　　*I. Tomson.* 910

The Louer compareth some subtile Suters
to the Hunter. To the tune of the Painter.

WHen as the Hunter goeth out,
　with hounds in brace.
　　　　C　　　　　　The 915

The Hart to hunt, and set about,
   with wilie trace,
He doth it more to see and view,
Her wilinesse (I tell you true.)   920
Her trips and skips, now here, now there,
With squats and flats, which hath no pere.
¶ More than to win or get the game
   to beare away:
He is not greedie of the same,   925
   (thus Hunters saie:
So some men hunt by hote desire,
To *Venus* Dames, and do require
With fauor to haue her, or els they wil die,
they loue her, & prooue her, and wot ye why? 930
¶ Forsooth to see her subtilnesse, & wily way,
Whē they (God knows) mean nothing lesse
   than they do say:
For when they see they may her win,
They leaue then where they did begin.   935
   they prate and make the matter nice,
     And leaue her in fooles paradice.
¶ Wherefore of such (good Ladie now)
   wisely beware,
Least flinging fancies in their brow,   940
   do breed you care:
And at the first giue them the checke,
Least they at last giue you the geck,
   And scornfully disdaine ye then,
     In faith there are such kind of men. 945
                  ¶ But

¶ But I am none of those indeed,
   beleeue me now:
I am your man if you me need,   950
   I make a vow:
To serue you without doublenesse:
With feruent heart my owne mistresse,
   Demaund me, commaund me,
   what please ye, and whan,   955
I wil be stil readie, as I am true man.

A new Sonet of Pyramus and Thisbie.
To the, Downe right Squier.

YOu Dames (I say) that climbe the
   of *Helicon*,   (mount   960
   Come on with me, and giue account,
   what hath been don:
Come tell the chaunce ye Muses all,
   and dolefull newes,
Which on these Louers did befall,   965
   which I accuse.
In *Babilon* not long agone,
   a noble Prince did dwell:
whose daughter bright dimd ech ones sight,
   so farre she did excel.   970
¶ An other Lord of high renowne,
   who had a sonne:
And dwelling there within the towne,
   great loue begunne:
Pyramus this noble Knight,   975
   I tel you true:
       C ii   Who

Who with the loue of *Thisbie* bright,
    did cares renue: 980
It came to passe, their secrets was,
    beknowne vnto them both:
And then in minde, they place do finde,
    where they their loue vnclothe.
¶ This loue they vse long tract of time,   985
    till it befell:
At last they promised to meet at prime,
    by *Minus* well:
Where they might louingly imbrace,
    in loues delight: 990
That he might see his *Thisbies* face,
    and she his sight:
In ioyful case, she approcht the place,
    where she her *Pyramus*
Had thought to viewd, but was renewd,   995
    to them most dolorous.
¶ Thus while she staies for *Pyramus*,
    there did proceed:
Out of the wood a Lion fierce,
    made *Thisbie* dreed: 1000
And as in haste she fled awaie,
    her Mantle fine:
The Lion tare in stead of praie,
    till that the time
That *Pyramus* proceeded thus,   1005
    and see how lion tare
The Mantle this of *Thisbie* his,
    he desperately doth fare.

                    ¶ For

¶ For why he thought the lion had,   1011
    faire *Thisbie* slaine.
And then the beast with his bright blade,
    he slew certaine:
Then made he mone and said alas,   1015
    (O wretched wight)
Now art thou in a woful case
    for *Thisbie* bright:
Oh Gods aboue, my faithfull loue
    shal neuer faile this need: 1020
For this my breath by fatall death,
    shal weaue *Atropos* threed.
¶ Then from his sheathe he drew his blade,
    and to his hart
He thrust the point, and life did vade,   1025
    with painfull smart:
Then *Thisbie* she from cabin came
    with pleasure great,
And to the well apase she ran,
    there for to treat: 1030
And to discusse, to *Pyramus*
    of al her former feares.
And when slaine she, found him truly,
    she shed foorth bitter teares.
¶ When sorrow great that she had made,   1035
    she took in hand
The bloudie knife, to end her life,
    by fatall band.
You Ladies all, peruse and see,
    the faithfulnesse,   1040

How these two Louers did agree,
   to die in distresse:
You Muses waile, and do not faile,   1045
   but still do you lament:
These louers twaine, who with such paine,
   did die so well content.
          Finis. I. Tomson.

A Sonet of a Louer in the praise of his lady.   1050
To Calen o Custure me: sung at euerie lines end.

WHē as I view your comly grace, *Ca. &c*
   Your golden haires, your angels face:
Your azured veines much like the skies,
Your siluer teeth, your Christall eies.   1055
   Your Corall lips, your crimson cheeks,
That Gods and men both loue and leekes.
¶ Your pretie mouth with diuers gifts,
Which driueth wise men to their shifts:
So braue, so fine, so trim, so yong,   1060
With heauenlie wit and pleasant tongue,
   That *Pallas* though she did excell,
   Could frame ne tel a tale so well.
¶ Your voice so sweet, your necke so white,
   your bodie fine and small in sight: 1065
Your fingers long so nimble be,
To vtter foorth such harmonie,
   As all the Muses for a space:
   To sit and heare do giue you place.
¶ Your pretie foot with all the rest,   1070
That may be seene or may be gest:
              Doth

Doth beare such shape, that beautie may
Giue place to thee and go her way: 1075
    And *Paris* nowe must change his doome,
    For *Venus* lo must giue thee roome.
¶ Whose gleams doth heat my hart as fier,
Although I burne, yet would I nier:
Within my selfe then can I say: 1080
The night is gone, behold the day:
    Behold the star so cleare and bright,
    As dimmes the sight of *Phœbus* light:
¶ Whose fame by pen for to discriue,
Doth passe ech wight that is aliue: 1085
Then how dare I with boldned face,
Presume to craue or wish your grace?
    And thus amazed as I stand,
    Not feeling sense, nor moouing hand.
¶ My soule with silence moouing sense,   1090
Doth wish of God with reuerence,
Long life, and vertue you possesse:
To match those gifts of worthinesse,
    And loue and pitie may be spide,
    To be your chief and onely guide.   1095

¶ *A proper Sonet, Intituled, Maid, wil you*
    marrie. To the Blacke Almaine.

Aid, wil you marie?   I pray sir tarie,
    I am not disposed to wed a:
    For he y̆ shal haue me, wil neuer de   1100
    he shal haue my maidêhed a.   (ny me
Why then you wil not wed me?
No sure sire I haue sped me,

You must go seeke some other wight,   1106
    That better may your heart delight.
For I am sped I tell you true,
beleeu me it greeus me, I may not haue you,
To wed you & bed you as a woman shold be   1110
¶ For if I could, be sure I would,
    consent to your desire:
I would not doubt, to bring about,
    ech thing you would require:
But promise now is made,   1115
Which cannot be staide;
    It is a womans honestie,
    To keep her promise faithfully.
And so I do meane til death to do,
Consider and gather, that this is true: 1120
Choose it, and vse it, the honester you.
¶ But if you seek, for to misleeke,
    with this that I haue done:
Or else disdaine, that I so plaine
    this talke with you haue begone: 1125
Farewell I wil not let you,
He fisheth wel that gets you.
    And sure I thinke your other friend,
    Will prooue a Cuckold in the end:
But he wil take heed if he be wise,   1130
To watch you & catch you, with *Argus* eies,
Besetting and letting your wonted guise.
¶ Although the Cat doth winke a while,
    yet sure she is not blinde:

                                              It   1135

It is the waie for to beguile,
   the Mice that run behind:
   And if she see them running,
Then straightway she is comming: 1140
    Vpon their head she claps her foote,
    To striue with her it is no boote.
The seelie poore Mice dare neuer play,
She catcheth and snatcheth them euery day,
Yet whip they, & skip they, whẽ she is away. 1145
¶ And if perhaps they fall in trap,
   to death then must they yeeld:
They were better thẽ, to haue kept their den
   than straie abroad the field:
But they that will be ranging,   1150
Shall soone repent their changing:
And so shall you ere it be long,
Wherefore remember well my song:
    And do not snuffe though I be plaine,
    But cherily, merily, take the same.   1155
    For huffing & snuffing deserueth blame.
¶ For where you say you must obay,
   the promise you haue made,
So sure as I wil neuer flie,
   from that I haue said: 1160
    Therefore to them I leaue you,
    Which gladly wil receiue you:
You must go choose some other mate,
According to your own estate.
    For I do meane to liue in rest,   1165

Go seek you, and leek you an other guest,
And choose him, and vse him, as you like best.

The ioy of Virginitie: to, The Gods of loue   1170

I Iudge and finde, how God doth minde,
　　to furnish, to furnish
　　　his heauenly throne aboue,
　　With virgins pure, this am I sure,
　　　without misse, without misse: 1175
　　　　with other Saints he doth loue:
It is allowed as you may reade,
And eke auowed by *Paul* indeede,
　　Virginitie is accepted,
　　　a thing high in Gods sight: 1180
Though marriage is selected,
　　a thing to be most right:
　　　yet must I praise *Virginitie*,
　　For I would faine a Virgin be.
¶ You Virgins pure, your selues assure,   1185
　　and credite, and credite:
　　　great ioy you shall possesse,
Which I (God knows) cannot disclose,
　　nor spreade it, nor spreade it,
　　　ne yet by pen expresse.   1190
Nor halfe the ioies that you shall finde,
I can not iudge for you assignde:
When hence your ghost shall yeelded be,
　　into the throne of blisse:
In chaste and pure Virginitie,   1195
　　for thought or deed ywisse:
　　　Wher you shal raign, with God on hie
　　　For euermore eternally.   And

¶ And when doubtlesse, you shal possesse, 1200
  with Iesus, with Iesus,
   these ioies celestiall.
Then Ladie Fame, wil blaze your name,
  amongst vs, amongst vs,
   which then on earth raigne shal. 1205
She wil resound in euerie coast,
By trumpet sound, and wil you boast?
  So that although you do depart
   This mortall life so vaine:
Your chastitie in euerie heart, 1210
  by memorie shall remaine.
But hard it is, I saie no more,
To finde an hundreth in a score. *Finis.*

¶ *A warning for Wooers, that they be not*
 ouer hastie, nor deceiued with womens 1215
 beautie. *To, Salisburie Plaine.*

YE louing wormes come learne of me
  The plagues to leaue that linked be:
  The grudge, the grief, the gret anoy,
  The fickle faith, the fading ioy: 1220
 in time, take heed,
In fruitlesse soile sow not thy seed:
  buie not, with cost,
  the thing that yeelds but labour lost.
¶ If *Cupids* dart do chance to light, 1225
So that affection dimmes thy sight,
Then raise vp reason by and by,
With skill thy heart to fortifie

       Wheer

Where is a breach,   1231
Oft times too late doth come the Leach:
   Sparks are put out,
      when fornace flames do rage about.
¶ Thine owne delay must win the field,   1235
When lust doth leade thy heart to yeeld:
When steed is stolne, who makes al fast,
May go on foot for al his haste:
   In time shut gate,
     For had I wist, doth come too late,   1240
      Fast bind, fast find,
       Repentance alwaies commeth behind.
¶ The *Syrens* times oft time beguiles,
So doth the teares of Crocodiles:
But who so learnes *Vlysses* lore,   1245
May passe the seas, and win the shore.
   Stop eares, stand fast,
Through *Cupids* trips, thou shalt him cast:
   Flie baits, shun hookes,
Be thou not snarde with louely lookes.   1250
¶ Where *Venus* hath the maisterie,
There loue hath lost her libertie:
where loue doth win the victorie,
The fort is sackt with crueltie.
   First look, then leap,   1255
In suretie so your shinnes you keepe:
   The snake doth sting,
   That lurking lieth with hissing.
¶ VVhere *Cupids* fort hath made a waie,
There graue aduise doth beare no swaie,   1260

                   where

Where Loue doth raigne and rule the roste,
There reason is exilde the coast:
Like all, loue none, except ye vse discretion.   1265
First try, thē trust, be not deceiued with sinful
¶ Marke *Priams* sonne, his fond deuise (lust,
When *Venus* did obtaine the price:
For *Pallas* skil and *Iunoes* strength,
He chose that bred his bane at length.   1270
Choos wit, leaue wil, let *Helen* be ẇ *Paris* stil:
Amis goeth al, wher fācie forceth fooles to fall.
¶ Where was there found a happier wight,
Than *Troylus* was til loue did light?
What was the end of *Romeus*.   1275
Did he not die like *Piramus*
who baths in blis? let him be mindful of *Iphis*
who seeks to plese, may riddē be like *Hercules*.
¶ I lothe to tel the peeuish brawles,
And fond delights of *Cupids* thrawles,   1280
Like momish mates of *Midas* mood,
They gape to get that doth no good: (Cup
Now down, now vp, as tapsters vse to tosse ỹ
One breedeth ioy, another breeds as great anoy
¶ Some loue for wealth, and some for hue,   1285
And none of both these loues are true.
For when the Mil hath lost hir sailes,
Then must the Miller lose his vailes:
    Of grasse commeth hay,
And flowers faire wil soon decay: 1290
    Of ripe commeth rotten,
     In age al beautie is forgotten.
               Some

Some loueth too hie, and some too lowe,   1295
And of them both great griefs do grow,
And some do loue the common sort:
And common folke vse common sport.
    Looke not too hie,
Least that a chip fall in thine eie: 1300
    But hie or lowe,
Ye may be sure she is a shrow.
¶ But sirs, I vse to tell no tales,
Ech fish that swims doth not beare scales,
In euerie hedge I finde not thornes: 1305
Nor euerie beast doth carrie hornes:
    I saie not so,
That euerie woman causeth wo:
    That were too broad,
Who loueth not venom must shun the tode.   1310
¶ Who vseth still the truth to tel,
May blamed be though he saie wel:
Say Crowe is white, and snowe is blacke,
Lay not the fault on womans backe,
Thousands were good,   1315
But few scapte drowning in *Noes* flood:
    Most are wel bent,
I must say so, least I be shent.   *Finis.*

    ¶ *An excellent Song of an outcast Louer.*
      To, All in a Garden green.   1320

MY fancie did I fixe,
    in faithful forme and frame:
    in hope ther shuld no blustring blast
    haue power to moue the same.
        ¶ And   1325

¶ And as the Gods do know,
  and world can witnesse beare:
I neuer serued other Saint,
  nor Idoll other where.   1330
¶ But one, and that was she,
  whom I in heart did shrine:
And made account that pretious pearle,
  and iewel rich was mine.
¶ No toile, nor labour great,   1335
  could wearie me herein:
For stil I had a *Iasons* heart,
  the golden fleece to win.
¶ And sure my sute was hearde,
  I spent no time in vaine: 1340
A grant of friendship at her hand,
  I got to quite my paine.
With solemne vowe and othe.
  was knit the True-loue knot,
And friendly did we treat of loue,   1345
  as place and time we got.
¶ Now would we send our sighes,
  as far as they might go,
Now would we worke with open signes,
  to blaze our inward wo.   1350
¶ Now rings and tokens too,
  renude our friendship stil,
And ech deuice that could be wrought,
  exprest our plaine goodwill,
True meaning went withall,   1355
  it cannot be denide:

                            Per-

Performance of the promise past,
 was hopte for of ech side: 1360
¶ And lookt for out of hand:
 such vowes did we two make,
As God himself had present been,
 record thereof to take.
¶ And for my part I sweare,   1365
 by all the Gods aboue,
I neuer thought of other friend,
 nor sought for other loue.
¶ The same consent in her,
 I saw ful oft appeare,   1370
If eies could see, or head could iudge,
 or eare had power to heare.
¶ Yet loe words are but winde,
 an other new come guest,
Hath won her fauour (as I feare)   1375
 as fancies rise in brest.
Her friend that wel deserues,
 is out of countenaunce quite,
She makes the game to see me shoot,
 while others hit the white.   1380
He may wel beat the bush,
 as manie thousands doo:
And misse the birds, and haply loose
 his part of feathers too.
¶ He hops without the ring,   1385
 yet daunceth on the trace,
When some come after soft and faire,
 a heauie hobling pace.

         ¶ In

¶ In these vnconstant daies,
    such troth these women haue: 1391
As wauering as the aspen leaf
    they are, so God me saue.
¶ For no deserts of men   1395
    are weid, what ere they be;
For in a mood their minds are led
    with new delights we see.
¶ The guiltlesse goeth to wrack,
    the gorgeous peacocks gay: 1400
They do esteem vpon no cause,
    and turne their friends away.
¶ I blame not al for one,
    some flowers grow by the weeds,
Some are as sure as lock and key,   1405
    and iust of words and deeds.
¶ And yet of one I waile,
    of one I crie and plaine:
And for her sake shall neuer none,
    so nip my heart againe: 1410
¶ If for offence or fault,
    I had been floong at heele:
The lesse had been my bitter smart,
    and gnawing greefe I feele.
¶ But being once reteind,   1415
    a friend by her consent:
And after that to be disdaind,
    when best good will I ment,
¶ I take it nothing well,
    for if my power could show,   1420

D   With

With Larum bel and open crie,
   the world should throughly know.

The complaint of a woman Louer,   1425
    To the tune of, Raging loue.

THough wisdom wold I should refrain,
  My heaped cares here to vnfold:
  Good Ladies yet my inward paine,
    So pricketh me I haue no holde: 1430
But that I must my griefe bewray,
Bedewed in teares with doleful tunes,
That you may heare, and after say,
Loe, this is she whom loue consumes.
¶ My grief doth grow by my desire.   1435
To fancie him that stormes my woe:
He naught regards my flaming fire,
Alas why doth he serue me so?
    Whose fained teares I did beleeue,
    And wept to heare his wailing voice,   1440
    But now, alas, too soon I preeue,
    Al men are false, there is no choice.
¶ Had euer woman such reward,
At anie time for her goodwill?
Had euer woman hap so hard,   1445
So cruelly for loue to spill?
    What paps (alas) did giue him food,
    That thus vnkindly workes my wo?
    What beast is of so cruell moode,
    to hate the hart that loues him so?   1450
¶ Like as the simple Turtle true,
In mourning groanes I spend the day:

               My

My daily cares night dooth renew, 1455
To thinke how he did me betray:
  And when my weary limmes wold rest,
 My sleepe vnsound hath dreadfull dreams,
Thus greeuous greefes my hart doth wrest
That stil mine eies run down like streams: 1460
¶ And yet, full oft it dooth me good,
To haunt the place where he hath beene,
To kisse the ground whereon he stoode,
When he (alas) my loue did win.
  To kisse the Bed wheron we laye? 1465
  Now may I thinke vnto my paine,
  O blisfull place full oft I say:
  Render to me my loue againe,
¶ But all is lost that may not be,
Another dooth possesse my right: 1470
His cruell hart, disdaineth me,
New loue hath put the olde, to flight:
  He loues to see my watered eyes,
  and laughes to see how I do pine:
  No words can well my woes comprise, 1475
  alas what griefe is like to mine?
¶ You comly Dams, beware by me,
To rue sweete words of fickle trust:
For I may well example be,
How filed talke oft prooues vniust 1480
  But sith deceipt haps to my pay,
  Good Ladyes helpe my dolefull tunes,
  That you may here and after say:
  Loe this is she whom loue consumes.
     D ij.   A 1485

*A proper sonet, Intituled: I smile to see how
you deuise.   To anie pleasant tune.*

I Smile to see how you deuise,
New masking nets my eies to bleare: 1490
your self you cannot so disguise:
But as you are, you must appeare.
¶ your priuie winkes at boord I see,
And how you set your rouing mind:
your selfe you cannot hide from me,   1495
Although I wincke, I am not blind.
¶ The secret sighs and fained cheare,
That oft doth paine thy carefull brest:
To me right plainly doth appeare,
I see in whom thy hart doth rest.   1500
¶ And though thou makest a fained vow,
That loue no more thy heart should nip,
yet think I know as well as thou,
The fickle helm doth guide the ship.
¶ The Salamander in the fire,   1505
By course of kinde doth bathe his limmes:
The floting Fish taketh his desire,
In running streams whereas he swimmes.
¶ So thou in change dost take delight,
Ful wel I know thy slipperie kinde: 1510
In vaine thou seemst to dim my sight,
Thy rowling eies bewraieth thy minde.
¶ I see him smile that doth possesse
Thy loue which once I honoured most:
If he be wise, he may well gesse,   1515
Thy loue soon won, wil soon be lost.

An[d]

¶ And sith thou canst no man intice,
That he should stil loue thee alone: 1520
Thy beautie now hath lost her price,
I see thy sauorie sent is gone.
¶ Therefore leaue off thy wonted plaie,
But, as thou art, thou wilt appeare,
Vnlesse thou canst deuise a waie, 1525
To dark the Sun that shines so cleare.
¶ And keep thy friend that thou hast won,
In trueth to him thy loue supplie,
Least he at length as I haue done,
Take off thy Belles and let thee flie. 1530

A Sonet of two faithfull Louers, exhorting
one another to be constant.
To the tune of Kypascie.

THe famous Prince of *Macedon*,
   whose wars increst his worthy name 1535
   Triumphed not so, when he had won
   By conquest great, immortall fame,
  As I reioice, reioice,
For thee, my choice, with heart and voice,
   Since thou art mine, 1540
Whom, long to loue, the Gods assigne.
¶ The secret flames of this my loue,
The stars had wrought ere I was borne,
Whose sugred force my hart doth moue,
And eke my will so sure hath sworne. 1545
  that Fortunes lore, no more,
  though I therefore, did life abhore:
  Shall neuer make,
Forgetful dewes my heat to slake.

                   If 1550

¶ If that I false my faith to thee,
Or seeke to chaunge for any newe:
If thoughts appeare so ill in me,
If thou thy life shall iustly rew.
Such kinde of woe, of woe:
As friende or foe, might to me showe:
Betide me than,
Or wurse, if it may hap to man.
¶ Then let vs ioy in this our loue:
In spite of Fortunes wrath, my deere:
Twoo willes in one, as dooth behooue,
One loue in both, let still appeare:
And I will be, will be,
Piramus to thee, my owne *Thisbie*,
So thou againe,
My constant louer shalt remaine.

A proper new Dity: Intituled Fie vpõ Loue and al his lawes. To the tune of lumber me.

SVch bitter fruict thy loue doth yeelde,
Such broken sleepes, such hope vnsure,
Thy call so oft hath me beguilde.
That I vnneth can well indure:
But crie (alas) as I haue cause,
Fie vpon Loue and all his Lawes.
¶ Like *Piramus*, I sigh and grone,
VVhom Stonie wals, keept from his loue,
And as the wofull *Palemon*,
A thousand stormes, for thee I prooue,
Yet thou a cruell Tigers whelpe,
All slaiest the hart, whom thou maist help.

[¶ A]

¶A craggie Rocke, thy Cradle, was,
And Tigers milke sure was thy foode,   1585
VVherby Dame Nature broought to passe,
That like the Nurse should be thy moode:
    VVild and vnkinde, cruell and fell,
    to rent the hart that loues thee well.
¶The Crocadile with fained teares,   1590
The Fisher not so oft beguiles:
As thou hast luld my simple eares,
To here sweet words, full fraught ẘ wiles,
    that I may say, as I doo prooue,
    VVo worth the time, I gan to loue.   1595
¶Sith thou hast vowd to worke my wrack,
And hast no will my wealth to way:
Farewell vnkinde, I will keepe backe,
Such toyes as may my helth decay:
    and still will cry as I haue cause.   1600
    Fie vpon Loue and all his lawes.

The Louer being wounded with his Ladis
beutie, requireth mercy.
To the tune of Apelles.

THe liuelie sparkes of those two eyes,   1605
  my wounded hart hath set on fire:
  And since I can no way deuise,
To stay the rage of my desire,
    with sighs and trembling tears I craue
    my deare on me some pitie haue.   1610
¶In vewing thee, I tooke such ioy,
As one that sought his quiet rest:
Vntill I felt the fethered boy,

                      Aye

Ay flickring in my captiue brest: 1616
   Since that time loe, in deepe dispaire,
   all voide of ioy, my time I weare.
¶ The wofull prisoner *Palemon,*
And *Troylus* eke kinge *Pyramus* sonne,   1620
Constrained by loue did neuer mone:
As I my deer for thee haue done.
   Let pitie then requite my paines,
My life and death in thee remaines.
¶ If constant loue may reape his hire,   1625
And faith vnfained may purchace:
Great hope I haue to my desire.
Your gentle hart wil grant me grace,
   Til then (my deer) in few words plaine,
   In pensiue thoughts I shall remaine.   1630

The lamentation of a woman being wrong-
fully defamed. To the tune of Damon & Pithias.

YOu Ladies falsly deemd,
   of anie fault or crime:
   Command your pensiue harts to help   1635
   this dolefull tune of mine:
For spiteful men there are,
   that faults would fain espie:
Alas, what heart would heare their talke,
   but willingly would die.   1640
¶ I waile oft times in woe,
   and curse mine houre of birth,
Such slanderous pangs do me oppresse,
   when others ioy in mirth:
              Belike   1645

Belike it was ordaind to be my destinie.
Alas what heart would heare their talk, &c.
¶ A thousand good women,
    haue guiltlesse been accusde: 1650
For verie spite, although that they,
    their bodies neuer abusde:
the godly *Susāna* accused was falsly. alas &c.
¶ The poisoned *Pancalier*,
    ful falsly did accuse   1655
The good Dutchesse of *Sauoy*,
    because she did refuse,
To grant vnto his loue,
    that was so vngodlie. Alas what, &c
¶ Such false dissembling men,   1660
    stoong with *Alectos* dart:
Must needs haue place to spit their spite,
    vpon some guiltlesse hart:
Therefore, I must be pleasde,
    that they triumph on me, Alas, &c.   1665
¶ Therefore, Lord, I thee pray,
    the like death downe to send,
Vpon these false suspected men,
    or else their minds t'amend:
As thou hast done tofore,   1670
    vnto these persons three. Alas what, &c.

*A proper Song, Intituled: Fain wold I haue
a pretie thing to give vnto my Ladie.
To the tune of lustie Gallant.*

¶ *Fain would I haue a pretie thing,*   1675
    to giue vnto my Ladie:
                I name

I name no thing, nor I meane no thing,
But as pretie a thing as may bee.   1680

TWentie iorneyes would I make,
  and twentie waies would hie me,
 To make aduenture for her sake,
  to set some matter by me:
But I would faine haue a pretie thing, &c,   1685
  I name nothing, nor I meane nothing, &c.
¶ Some do long for pretie knackes,
  and some for straunge deuices:
God send me that my Ladie lackes,
  I care not what the price is, thus faine, &c 1690
¶ Some goe here, and some go there,
  wheare gases be not geason:
And I goe gaping euery where,
  but still come out of season.   Yet faine, &c,
¶ I walke the towne, and tread the streete,   1695
  in euery corner seeking:
The pretie thinge I cannot meete,
  thats for my Ladies liking.   Faine, &c.
¶ The Mercers pull me going by,
  the Silkie wiues say, what lacke ye?   1700
The thing you haue not, then say I.
  ye foolish fooles, go packe ye.   But fain &c.
¶ It is not all the Silke in Cheape,
  nor all the golden treasure:
Nor twentie Bushels on a heape,   1705
  can do my Ladie pleasure.   But faine, &c.
¶ The Grauers of the golden showes,
  with Iuelles do beset me.

       The

The Shemsters in the shoppes that sowes,   1711
    they do nothing but let me: But faine, &c.
¶ But were it in the wit of man,
    by any meanes to make it,
I could for Money buy it than,   1715
    and say, faire Lady, take it. Thus, fain, &c.
¶ O Lady, what a lucke is this:
    that my good willing misseth:
To finde what pretie thing it is,
    that my good Lady wisheth.   1720
Thus fain wold I haue had this preti thing
    to giue vnto my Ladie:
I said no harme, nor I ment no harme,
    but as pretie a thing as may be.

    A proper wooing Song, intituled: Maide   1725
        will ye loue me: ye or no?
    To the tune of the Marchaunts Daughter
        went ouer the fielde.

MAyde will ye loue me yea or no?
    tell me the trothe, and let me goe.   1730
    It can be no lesse then a sinfull deed,
        trust me truely,
To linger a Louer that lookes to speede,
    in due time duely.
¶ You Maids that thinke your selus as fine,   1735
As *Venus* and all the Muses nine:
The Father himselfe whē he first made mā
        trust me truely:
Made you for his help whē the world began
    in due time duely.   1740
              [Then]

¶ Then sith Gods wil was euen so.
Why should you disdaine you Louer tho?
But rather with a willing heart,   1745
        Loue him truely?
For in so doing, you do but your part,
        Let reason rule ye.
¶ Consider (sweet) what sighs and sobbes,
Do nip my heart with cruell throbbes,   1750
And al (my deer) for the loue of you,
        Trust me truly:
But I hope that you wil some mercie show,
        In due time duely.
¶ If that you do my case well way,   1755
And shew some signe whereby I may
Haue some good hope of your good grace,
        Trust me truely:
I count my selfe in a blessed case,
        Let reason rule ye.   1760
¶ And for my part, whilst I do liue,
To loue you most faithfully, my hãd I giue,
Forsaking all other, for your sweet sake,
        Trust me truly:
In token whereof, my troth I betake,   1765
        to your selfe most duely.
¶ And though for this time we must depart,
yet keep you this ring tru token of my hart,
Til time do serue, we meet againe,
        Let reason rule ye.   1770
Whẽ an answer of cõfort, I trust to obtain,
        In due time duly.
                Now

Now must I depart with sighing teares,   1775
With sobbing heart and burning eares:
Pale in the face, and faint as I may,
    trust me truly:
But I hope our next meeting, a ioyfull day,
    in due time duly.   1780

The painefull plight of a Louer oppressed
with the beautifull looks of his Lady.
To the tune of, I loued her ouer wel.

WHĕ as thy eies, ẙ wretched spies
    did breed my cause of care: 1785
    And sisters three did full agree,
        my fatall threed to spare.
Then let these words ingrauen be,
    on toomb whereas I lie,
    That here lies one whom spiteful loue,   1790
    hath caused for to die.
¶ Somtimes I spend the night to end,
    in dolors and in woe:
Somtime againe vnto my pain,
    my chiefest ioy doth grow.   1795
    When as in minde, thy shape I finde,
        as fancie doth me tell:
    Whome nowe I knowe, as proofe doth
        I loued thee ouer wel.   (show
¶ How oft within my wreathed arme,   1800
    desired I to folde:
Thy Christall corps, of whom I ioyed,
    more dearer than of golde.
                But

But now disdaine, dooth breede my paine,   1806
    and thou canst not denie:
But that I loued thee ouer well:
    that caused me to die.
The hound that serues his Maisters will,   1810
    in raunging here and there,
The moyling Horse, that labours still,
    his burthen great to beare:
      In lew of paine, receiues againe,
        of him which did him owe: 1815
      As Natures heast, wiles most & least
        them thankefull for to showe.
¶ The Lyon and the Tyger fierce,
    as Nature doth them binde:
For loue, like loue repay againe: 1820
    in Stories we doo finde:
      Those beasts & birds both wild & tame,
        of frendships lore can tell:
      But thy reply, willes me to die.
        that loued thee ouer well.   1825
¶ Therfore, my deare and Darling faire,
    ensample take by those,
Which equally with loue againe,
    their louing mindes dispose:
      And giue him glee, whose death we s[ee]   1830
        approcheth very nie:
      Without he gaine, to ease his paine,
        which loued thee hartely.
¶ Then shall they say that see the same,
    where euer that they goe: 1835
              And

And wish for ay, as for thy pay,
    all *Nestors* yeares to know:
And I no lesse then all the rest,   1840
    should wish thee health for aye:
Because thou hast heard my request,
    and saued me from decay.

    A faithfull vow of two constant Louers
       To the new Rogero.   1845

SHall distance part our loue,
    or daily choice of chaunge?
Or sprites below, or Gods aboue,
    haue power to make vs straunge:
¶ No nothing here on earth,   1850
    that kinde hath made or wrought,
Shall force me to forget.
    goodwill so dearely bought,
¶ And for my part I vow,
    to serue for terme of life: 1855
Which promise may compare with her,
    which was *Vlisses* wife.
¶ Which vow if I doo breake,
    let vengeance on me fall,
Eche plague that on the earth may raigne,   1860
    I aske not one, but all.
¶ Though time may breede suspect,
    to fill your hart with toyes:
And absence may a mischefe breede,
    to let your wished ioyes: 1865
¶ Yet thinke I haue a troth,
    and honesty to keepe:

                     And

And weigh the time your loue hath dwelt,   1870
    within my hart so deep.
¶ And peise the words I spake,
    and marke my countenance then:
And let not slip no earnest sigh,
    if thou remember can.   1875
¶ At least forget no teares,
    that trickled downe my face:
And marke howe oft I wroong your hand,
    and blushed all the space.
¶ Remember how I sware,   1880
    and strook therewith my brest:
In witnesse when thou partst me fro,
    my heart with thee should rest.
¶ Thinke on the eger lookes,
    full loth to leaue thy sight,   1885
That made the signes when that she list,
    to like no other wight.
¶ If this be out of thought,
    yet call to minde againe,
The busie sute, the much adoe,   1890
    the labour and the paine,
¶ That at the first I had,
    ere thy good will I gate:
And think how for thy loue [al]one,
    I purchase partly hate.   1895
¶ But all is one with me,
    my heart so setled is:
No friend, nor foe, nor want of wealth,
    shall neuer hurt in this.

                            Be   1900

¶ Be constant now therefore,
  and faithfull to the end?
Be carefull how we both may do,
  to be ech others friend.   1905
¶ With free and cleane consent,
  two hearts in one I knit:
Which for my part, I vow to keep,
  and promise not to flit,
¶ Now let this vow be kept,   1910
  exchange thy heart for mine:
So shal two harts be in one breast,
  and both of them be thine.

A sorrowfull Sonet, made by M. George
  Mannington, at Cambridge Castle.   1915
  To the tune of Labandala Shot.

I Waile in wo, I plunge in pain,
  with sorowing sobs, I do complain,
 With wallowing waues I wish to die,
  I languish sore whereas I lie,   1920
In feare I faint in hope I holde,
With ruthe I runne, I was too bolde:
As lucklesse lot assigned me,
  in dangerous dale of destinie:
Hope bids me smile, Feare bids me weep,   1925
  My seelie soule thus Care doth keep.
¶ Yea too too late I do repent,
  the youthful yeares that I haue spent,
The retch lesse race of carelesse kinde,
  which hath bewitcht my woful minde.   1930
      E   [Such]

Such is the chaunce, such is the state,
Of those that trust too much to fate.
No bragging boast of gentle blood,   1935
What so he be, can do thee good:
    No wit, no strength, nor beauties hue,
    No friendly sute can death eschue.
¶ The dismall day hath had his wil,
And iustice seekes my life to spill: 1940
Reuengement craues by rigorous law,
Whereof I little stood in awe:
    The dolefull doom to end my life,
    Bedect with care and worldlie strife:
And frowning iudge hath giuen his doome.   1945
O gentle death thou art welcome:
    The losse of life, I do not feare,
    Then welcome death, the end of care.
¶ O prisoners poore, in dungeon deep,
Which passe the night in slumbring sleep: 1950
Wel may you rue your youthful race.
And now lament your cursed cace.
    Content your selfe with your estate,
    Impute no shame to fickle fate:
With wrong attempts, increase no wealth,   1955
Regard the state of prosperous health:
    And think on me, when I am dead:
    Whom such delights haue lewdly led.
¶ My friend and parents, where euer you be
Full little do you thinke on me: 1960
My mother milde, and dame so deer:
Thy louing childe, is fettred heer:

                      Would

Would God I had, I wish too late,   1965
   Been bred and borne of meaner estate:
Or else, would God my rechlesse eare,
Had been obedient for to heare,
   Your sage aduice and counsel true:
   But in the Lord parents adue.   1970
¶ You valiant hearts of youthfull train,
Which heard my heauie heart complain:
A good example take by me,
Which runne the race where euer you be:
   trust not too much to bilbow blade,   1975
   nor yet to fortunes fickle trade.
Hoist not your sailes no more in winde,
Least that some rocke, you chaunce to finde,
   or else be driuen to *Lybia* land,
   whereas the Barque may sinck in sand.   1980
¶ You students all that present be,
To view my fatall destinie,
would God I could requite your pain,
wherein you labour, although in vain,
   if mightie God would think it good,   1985
   to spare my life and vitall blood,
For this your profered curtesie,
I would remaine most stedfastly,
   Your seruant true in deed and word,
   But welcome death, as please the Lord.   1990
¶ Yea welcome death, the end of woe,
And farewell life, my fatall foe:
Yea welcome death, the end of strife,
Adue the care of mortall life,
        E ii   For   1995

For though this life doth fleet away,
In heauen I hope to liue for ay:
A place of ioy and perfect rest,
Which Christ hath purchaste for the best: 2000
    Til that we meet in heauen most hiest:
    Adue, farewell in Iesu Christ.

*A proper Sonet, of an vnkinde Damsell, to
to her faithful Louer. To, the nine Muses.*

THe ofter that I view and see,   2005
    That plesant face and faire beautie,
        whereto my heart is bound:
    The neer my Miftresse is to me,
My health is farthest off I see:
    and fresher is my wound: 2010
Like as the flame doth quench by fire,
    or streams consume by raigne,
So doth the sight that I desire,
    appease my grief and paine:
Like a flie that doth hie,   2015
    and haste into the fire:
So in brief, findes her grief,
    that thought to sport aspire.
¶ When first I saw those Christal streams,
I little thought on beauties beams: 2020
    sweet venom to haue found,
But wilful wil did prick me foorth,
Perforce to take my grief in woorth,
    that causd my mortall wound:
And *Cupid* blind compeld me so,   2025
    my fruitlesse hope to hide:
                    Wherein

Wherein remaind my bitter wo:
   thus stil he did me guide: 2030
Then his dart, to my hart,
   he slung with cruell fist:
Whose poison fel, I know right wel,
   no louer may resist.
¶ Thus vainly stil, I frame my sute, 2035
Of ill sowen seeds, such is the frute,
   experience doth it show:
The fault is hers the pain is mine,
And thus my sentence I define,
   I hapned on a shrow: 2040
And now beware, ye yongmen all,
     Example take by mee:
Least beauties bait in *Cupids* thrall,
   do catch you priuily:
So stay you, I pray you, 2045
   and marke you my great wrong,
Forsaken, not taken,
   thus end I now my song.

   The Louer complaineth the absence of
    his Ladie, wisheth for death. 2050
     To, the new Almaine.

SIth spitefull spite hath spide her time,
   my wished ioies to end:
  And drowping dread hath driuen me
   from my new chosen friend: (now 2055
I can but waile the want,
   of this my former ioie:
Sith spiteful force hath sought so long,
   my blisse for to annoie.
            ¶ B 2060

¶ But though it be our chance
    asunder for to be,
My heart in pawne til we do meet,
    Shal stil remaine with thee: 2065
      And then we shall renue,
      our sugred pleasures past:
And loue that loue, that seekes no change,
    whilst life in vs do last.
¶ Perhaps my absence may,   2070
    or else some other let:
By choice of change, cause thee my deer,
    our former loue forget:
      And thou renounce the oth,
        which erst thou vowdst to me: 2075
My deerest blood in recompence,
    thou sure shouldst shortly see.
A thousand sighs to sēd to thee I wil not let,
Ne to bewaile the losse of thee, I neuer will
    But stil suppose I see,   (forget 2080
    the same before my face:
And louingly between my armes,
    thy corps I do embrace.
¶ Thus feed I fancie stil,
    for lacke of greater ioy: 2085
With such like thoughts, which daily doth,
    my wofull heart annoy:
      thus stil in hope I liue,
        my wished ioies to haue:
And in dispaire oft time I wish,   2090
    my feeble Corps in graue.
                       This

¶ This is the life I leade, til I thee see again
And so wil do, til dreadful death,   2095
   do seek to ease my paine,
whō rather I do wish, by force to end in wo,
   than for to liue in happie state,
    thy loue for to forgo.
¶ And thus farewell my deer,   2100
   with whom my heart shall rest,
Remember him that this did write,
   sith he doth loue thee best:
    And wil til greedie death,
     my daies do shorten now: 2105
Farewel my dear, loe here my faith
   and troth to thee I vow.   *Finis.*

The Louer compareth him self to the pain-
ful Falconer. To the tune, I loued her ouer wel.

THe soaring hawk from fist that flies,   2110
   her Falconer doth constraine:
   Sometime to range the ground vn-
    to find her out againe: (known,
And if by sight or sound of bell,
   his falcon he may see: 2115
wo ho he cries, with cheerful voice,
   the gladdest man is he.
¶ By Lure then in finest sort,
   he seekes to bring her in:
But if that she, ful gorged be,   2120
   he can not so her win:
Although her becks and bending eies,
   she manie proffers makes:

                      WO

Wo ho ho he cries, awaie she flies,   2126
    and so her leaue she takes.
¶ This wofull man with wearie limmes,
    runnes wandring round about:
At length by noise of chattering Pies,   2130
    his hawke againe found out
His heart was glad his eies had seen,
    his falcon swift of flight:
Wo ho ho he cries, she emptie gorgde,
    vpon his Lure doth light.   2135
¶ How glad was then the falconer there,
    no pen nor tongue can tel:
He swam in blisse that lately felt
    like paines of cruel hel.
His hand somtime vpon her train,   2140
    somtime vpon her brest:
Wo ho ho he cries with chearfull voice,
    his heart was now at rest.
¶ My deer likewise, beholde thy loue,
    what paines he doth indure: 2145
And now at length let pitie moue,
    to stoup vnto his Lure.
A hood of silk, and siluer belles,
    new gifts I promise thee:
Wo ho ho, I crie, I come then saie,   2150
    make me as glad as hee.

FINIS.

FRAGMENT OF ANOTHER EDITION OF
THE *HANDFUL*

THIS single leaf, corresponding to lines 1581–1645 of the *Handful of Pleasant Delights*, was found by J. W. Ebsworth among John Bagford's collection of early printed matter at the British Museum. The press-mark is 643. m. 9 (83). Ebsworth reprinted the leaf in his *Bagford Ballads*, 1878, I, 41 f., and Arber in his edition of the *Handful*, pp. xv f. In both reprints the contractions are expanded, lines are re-arranged, and the stanzas are normalized so that the early date of the leaf is obscured. Ebsworth, to be sure, believed that it was earlier in date than the *Handful*.

The typography itself seems to show that the leaf belongs to the third quarter of the sixteenth century and, therefore, that it antedated the 1584 *Handful*. Taken in connection with the Stationers' entry of 1566 and with the early dates of most of the ballads that appear in the *Handful*, it seems highly probable that the leaf actually came from the first edition of the *Pleasant Sonnets* in 1566. See the discussion on pages x–xiii, above.

The following misprints occur in this fragment:

  2 flayest (*read* slayest)
  8 flay (*read* slay)
 39 *Pryamus*, (*read* Pryamus son,)
 61 oft times (*text perhaps* ofttimes)

The chief verbal differences (ignoring mere spelling) between the fragment and the corresponding lines of the *Handful* are:

  6 thy Nurse: 1587 the Nurse
  8 flay: 1589 rent
 11 fild: 1592 luld
 55 Constraine: 1635 Command

All flayest the heart, whom thou maist help,
¶ A craggie Rock thy cradle was,
And Tygres milke sure was thy food:
Whereby Dame Nature brought to passe,   5
That like thy Nurse should be thy moode,
    Wilde and vnkind, cruell and fell.
        To flay the heart that loues thee well.
¶ The Crocodile with fained teares,
The Fisher not so oft beguiles: 10
As thou haste fild my simple eares,
To heare sweet words, full fraught with wiles
    That I may say, as I doo prooue,
        Wo worth the time I gan to loue.
¶ Sith thou haste vow'd to worke my wracke,   15
And haste no will my wealth to way,
Farewell vnkind, I will keepe backe
Such toyes as may my health decay:
    And still will crie, as I haue cause,
    Fie vpon loue and all his lawes.   20

The Louer being wounded with his Ladies
beautie, requireth mercy. To
the tune of Apelles.

THe liuely sparkes of those two eyes,
    My wounded heart hath set on fire: 25
    And since I can no way deuise,
    To stay the rage of my desire:
    with sighes and trembling teares I craue
    My deare, on me some pitty haue,
¶ In viewing thee, I tooke such ioy,   30
As one that sought his quiet rest:
        D 2   Vntil

Vntill I felt the feathered boy,
Ay flickering in my captiue breast: 35
    Since that time loe, in deep dispaire,
    All voyd of ioy, my time I weare,
¶ The wofull prisoner *Palemon,*
And *Troylus* eke, King *Pryamus,*
Constrain'd by loue did neuer mone,   40
As I (my deare) for the haue done,
    Let pitie then requite my paines
    My life and death in thee remaines.
¶ If constant loue may reape his hire,
And faith vnfained may purchase,   45
Great hope I haue to my desire,
Your gentle heart will grant me grace,
   Till then (my deare) in few words plaine,
    In pensiue thoughts I shall remaine.

The lamentation of a woman being wrongful-   50
   lie defamed.   To the tune of Damon and
          Pythias.

Y Ou Ladies falselie deem'd
   of any fault or crime,
Constraine your pensiue heartes to help   55
   this dolefull tune of mine:
For spitefull men there are,
   That faults would faine espie:
Alas, what heart would heare their talke,
   but willinglie would die: 60
¶ I waile oft times in woe,
   And curse mine houre of birth:
Such slanderous pangs doe me oppresse,
   when others ioy in mirth,   B[elike]

LIST OF MISPRINTS AND VARIANT READINGS

THIS list enumerates: (1) every misprint in the 1584 *Handful of Pleasant Delights* (*H*) except errors of punctuation, which I have left unchanged in the text; (2) every variation (and each is unintentional) from *H* in Crossley's edition for the Spenser Society (*S*); (3) every variation from *H* in Arber's edition (*A*) except words that Arber modernized by brackets or contractions that he expanded; and (4) a few variations in Park's edition (*P*). The last edition is too hopelessly inaccurate to deserve fuller citation. A glance through the list shows that *S* is not altogether successful as an exact reprint of *H* and that *A* is less carefully revised than is customary in Arber's work. References are to lines as numbered in the present edition.

I. The Printer to the Reader
  5 m[ight] *A: m. (though the period may be a broken i)*
    H: may P, S
  9 pleasant *A:* pleasaut *H, S*
  19 regard *A:* regnrd *H, S*

II. Text of the "Sonnets"
  67 [Le]tting: tting *H, S, A. Apparently* Le *was dropped from the form in printing*
  104 vse, *H, S:* vse. *A*
  188 purchase *A:* purchasr *H, S*
  203 now *S, A:* uow *H*
  210 sometimes *A:* sometlmes *H, S*
  279 be, *H, S:* be. *A, but the period is imperfect*
  350 wooed *S, A: H is badly blurred, type broken*
  357 her, *H, S:* hr, *A*
  385 will *A*
  386 as (the first one): ss *H, S:* so *A*
  403 Beauties *A:* Bꝛauties *H, S*

480 to *A:* so *H, S*

496 be ware *S, and there may be a slight separation in H*

560 not *A:* no₁ *H, S*

596 [Thy] *trimmed off in H. Only the top of the* T *remains. S has* Thy

628 [Faire] *entirely cut off, though S has* Faire

649 griefe *A*

724 [Mar-] *entirely cut off, though S has* Mar-

736 race. *A*

751 hugie *S, A:* bugie *H, P*

756 *S has* Abroad; *in H all but the top is cut off*

791 My *A:* (My *S, and so possibly H, but the parenthesis is, if intended, badly broken*

794 Narcissus *S, A:* Narcislus *H*

809 go, *A:* go. *S, H, but the dot in H is very small*

815 la[dy] *A:* la *H, S*

824 mercie *S, A:* merrie *H*

840 *Cecilia A*

856 'No, *A*

864 ioy, *S:* ioy. *A, and possibly H*

892 Wel *A:* Wil *H, S*

931 way. *A:* way, *S, and apparently H, but the mark is blurred*

959 Ou *A:* YOu *H, S*

971 renowne, *S, A:* reuowne, *H*

1008 fare, *S:* fare. *A, H, but the period in H may be a bad comma*

1038 band. *H:* hand. *P, S, A*

1096 *you S, A:* yon *H*

1097 To *A:* ᴛᴏ *H, S*

1100 deny *A:* de ny *H,S*   1103 sir *A*

1109 beleue *A,* greues *A*

1113 about *A*

1117 is *S, A:* i s *H*

1127 well *A,* you, *A*

1139 running, *S, A:* runniug, *H*

1216 *beautie, A*
1230 *Sonets S: onets H*
1263 rule *S, A:* rnle *H*
1286 true. *S, A:* trne. *H*
1317 bent, *S, A:* bcnt, *H, or else the* e *is broken*
1333 make *A:* made *H, S*
1338 to *S, A:* io *H*
1373 wordes *A*
1381 may *A:* way *H, S*
1394 saue. *S, A:* sane. *H*
1427 shold *A*
1451 true *S, A:* trne *H*
1454 *sundrie S:* s ⩵drie *H*
1466 thinke *S, A:* thiuke *H*
1467 blisfull *A, S: H apparently* blissull
1517 An[d] *H is torn and blurred. S has* And
1531 *faithfuli H* 1546 more. *A*
1555 rew, *S, and the point in H may be a bad comma*
1568 *Intituled. H, S: Intituled A*
1579 prooue *S, A:* proone *H*
1582 [¶ A] *H is torn, and only the top of the ¶ remains. S has* A
1592 simpie eares, *A and the fragment printed on page* 73. *H is too blurred to decipher. P has* sleep to cares; *S* stinted eares,
1595 gan *H?, the fragment (cf. p.* 73), *and A:* give *S*
1610 pity *S*
1653 accusde *A.* &c.*H apparently* &c'.
1653 falsly *S, A:* falsly. *H, though the period is very dim*
1657 refuse. *S, A:* refuse, *H, apparently, though the comma is broken*
1659 &c. *S, A:* &c *H*
1673 my *A:* ɯy *H, S*
1679 Inane *H no* (first one) *A, S:* uo *H*
1685 &c. *S:* &c, *H, A*
1690 &c. *S:* &c *H, A*

1691 goe (second one) *A:* go *H, S*
1694 &c. *A, S:* &c, *H, or else the comma is a blurred period*
1701 I, *S, A:* I. *H, or else the period is a broken comma*
1727 Marchaunts *H* (*though the first a is badly blurred, perhaps broken*), *S:* Mirchaunts *A*
1729 MAyde: *the* A *is broken in H*
1741 [Then] *cut off in H:* Then *S*
1775 sighingteares *H*
1814 receiues *A, S, but in H the blurred or broken type makes the spelling doubtful*
1816 wiles: *H is too badly blurred to be certain*
1817 thaukefull *H*
1822 birds, *S*
1824 die, *S*
1830 see *S:* s *H:* s[ee] *A*   1833 loued *S, A:* loned *H*
1834 they: th[e]y *A:* thy *H, S*
1853 good will *S*
1854 any *A:* my *H, S*
1866 troth, *S, A:* ttoth, *H*
1874 ernest *A*
1894 [al]one, *H is torn:* alone, *S, A*
1916 *tune A:* tnne *H, S*
1931 [Such] *not in H or S*
1945 frowning *S, A:* frowuing *H*
2001 hiest: *H, A:* blest: *S*
2003–4 *to to H, S, A*
2016 into *S, A:* iuto *H*
2030 thus *A:* hthus *H, S*
2030 guide r *H:* guide; *S:* guide? *A*
2032 flung *S:* slung *H, A*
2060 ¶ B: u B *H, S*
2077 shouldst *S, A:* shonldst *H*
2080 still *A*
2109 *Falconer. S, A:* Falcouer. *H*
2109 *To A:* ᴛᴏ *H, S*
2125 *Histories, H:* Histories. *S*
2126 flies, *S, A:* flies *H*

NOTES

*For words and phrases on which no notes are given,
see the Glossarial Index.*

*In the Notes the following works are cited by brief
titles or abbreviations: —*

Arber = *A Transcript of the Registers of the Company of
Stationers of London; 1554–1640*, edited by Edward Arber,
5 vols., London, 1875–1894.

Chappell, William. *Popular Music of the Olden Time*,
2 vols., London, n. d.

Collier, J. P. *Extracts from the Registers of the Stationers'
Company* [1557–1587], 2 vols., Shakespeare Society, London, 1848–1849.

Collmann, Herbert L. *Ballads and Broadsides, Chiefly of
the Elizabethan Period*, Roxburghe Club, 1912. [The so-
called Heber ballads reprinted in this book are now owned by
Mr. Henry E. Huntington.]

Gorgeous Gallery = J. P. Collier's reprint (1867) of *A
gorgious Gallery of Gallant Inuentions . . . ioyned together
and builded vp: By T. P.* [Thomas Proctor.] Imprinted at
London, for Richard Iones. 1578.

Lilly's *Ballads* = *A Collection of Seventy-Nine Black-
Letter Ballads and Broadsides, Printed in the Reign of Queen
Elizabeth*, London, 1867. [Joseph Lilly wrote the Preface
and printed the book.]

MS. Ashmole 48 = *Songs and Ballads, With Other Short
Poems, Chiefly of the Reign of Philip and Mary.* Edited from
a Manuscript in the Ashmolean Museum, by Thomas Wright,
Roxburghe Club, 1860.

MS. Cotton Vespasian A. XXV. The ballads from this
MS. are reprinted by K. Boeddeker in the *Jahrbuch für
romanische und englische Sprache*, Neue Folge, vols. II and
III.

N. E. D. = *The New English Dictionary.*

Paradise = J. P. Collier's reprint (1867) of *The Paradyse of daynty deuises. . . . Devised and written for the most part, by M. Edwardes. . . .* Imprinted at London, by Henry Disle, . . . 1578.

Pleasant Sonnets. The 1566 edition of the *Handful of Pleasant Delights.* See the discussion in the Introduction, pp. x–xiii, above.

The Printer to the Reader (Page 2)

6. *here may you wish and haue.* 'In this book you may have such pleasing songs as you may wish for, or desire.'

10. *lightly.* Easily; practically equivalent to 'as you are at all likely to crave.'

No. 1, Line 1

A book called *a nose gaye* was licensed to John King in 1557 (Arber, I, 75), and Collier (*Extracts*, I, 3) suggested that the "book" was really the present ballad. That identification, however, is too doubtful to be accepted. Probably No. 1 was the ballad called "A Smellinge Nosegaye" that John Cherlewood registered on January 15, 1582 (Arber, II, 406), though that title is equally applicable to "A pleasant Poesie, or sweete Nosegay of fragrant smellyng Flowers gathered in the Garden of heauenly Pleasure, the holy and blessed Bible" (Lilly's *Ballads*, p. 5). If No. 1 and "A Smellinge Nosegaye" were identical, it of course follows that No. 1 was not in the *Pleasant Sonnets* of 1566. Naturally enough, an Elizabethan printer would have begun a second edition of his miscellany with a new ballad.

From some edition of the *Handful* this ballad was liberally plagiarized by the author of "The Flattering Louers farewell to his Loue Nanny. To the tune of *Virginia*," a ballad in the Pepys Collection (I, 332) which Edward Wright printed about 1620. The following stanzas from the second part of the Pepys ballad (called "The Comfortable answere of *Nanny*") may be quoted for illustration:

[11]

Though Fortune do not fauour me,
    according to my will:
The proofe of my behauiour,
    is for to loue you still,

[12]

Intending not to change,
    so long as life doth last:
But in thy youth to run thy race,
    till youthfull daies be past.

[16]

But time is for to try,
    which needs be tryed must:
Hoping in God, while life doth last,
    you wil be true and iust.

[19]

Lauender is for Louers true,
    whiche I doe meane to keepe:
Rosemary for remembrance,
    till we againe doe meete.

[20]

Carnations is for graciousnes,
    marke this well by the way:
Giue no regard to flatterers,
    nor passe not what they say.

No. 1 was reprinted for the first time in Thomas Evans's
Old Ballads, 1810, I, 1. Mrs. C. C. Stopes, who reprinted it,
from Malone's manuscript copy, in her *William Hunnis* (1910,
pp. 307 ff., and cf. 206 ff.), thinks it may be the *Nosegay* that
Thomas Newton ascribes to Hunnis in his *Hive full of Honey*
(1578).

3. *fairings.* Presents given at or brought from a fair.
Ballads of advice or admonition were favorite fairings.

20. *flower his.* Flower's (possessive case). Cf. line 132.

21. *Lauander.* "Lauender alures the lookers eyes," —
Paradise, p. 87. Cf. line 31, note.

31. *Rosemarie is for remembrance.* Ophelia (*Hamlet*, IV, v, 174 ff.), commentators agree, quotes this passage: "There's rosemary, that's for remembrance; pray, love, remember; and there is pansies, that's for thoughts. . . . There's fennel for you." Cf. Drayton's *Ninth Eclogue:*

> He from his lass him lavender hath sent,
> Shewing her love, and doth requital crave;
> Him rosemary his sweet-heart, whose intent
> Is that he her should in remembrance have.

A somewhat similar passage dealing with pansies and columbines is in Chapman's *All Fools*, II, i, 232 ff. See also John Ingram's *Flora Symbolica*, pp. 200 ff.

39. *Sage is for sustenance.* "Cowley ascribes to *sage* the virtues here attributed to *rosemary*, and from its strengthening and bracing powers, infers its high reputation among medicaments for the memory. See his first book of Herbs" (Park's note). In *Muiopotmos* (1590), line 187, Spenser speaks of "the wholsome saulge." Cf. the old medical maxim, "Cur moriatur homo dum salvia crescit in horto?"

41. *stil lie.* That is, always, continually (as in lines 43, 75). *Continually* in line 42 is redundant.

47. *Fenel.* The *Paradise*, p. 86, describes fennel as "more fit, for some vnfrendly gest."

59. *And wil continue.* The sense is, 'and hoping that you will continue.'

65. *Time.* Thyme. The author is obviously punning on the proverb, "Time [not *thyme*] trieth all things" (Hazlitt's *English Proverbs*, 1882, p. 419).

81. *Ieliflowers.* Gillyflowers. "Some ioly youth the Gelliflower estemeth for his ioye," — *Paradise*, p. 87.

103. *I do not care.* 'I feel no anxiety.'

104. *stil vse, That.* 'Still conduct myself so that.'

115. *Cowsloppes is for counsell.* That is, cowslips are for secrets, or secrecy. Of cowslips the *Paradise*, p. 86, says, "Sometymes thei seme to coy."

123. *I pray.* *Read* ¶ I pray.
132. *he, his.* Referring to the nosegay.

No. 2, Line 134

Though not registered at Stationers' Hall, this ballad was probably printed by 1566. Such a date is indicated by the tune, *Downright squire* (used also for No. 13), as this tune was well known and popular in and shortly before 1566. It occurs, for example, as the tune of a ballad in MS. Ashmole 48 (ed. Wright, p. 191), a manuscript that was certainly compiled before that year ended (cf. my notes in *Modern Language Notes*, XXXIV [1919], 340–351). It is used also for an early ballad in Lilly's *Ballads*, p. 105.

L. Gibson, the author, signed his name as Leonarde Gybson to "A very proper Dittie: To the tune of Lightie Loue" (Lilly's *Ballads*, p. 113). His *Tower of Trustinesse*, a work in prose and verse, is dated 1555 in Lilly's *Ballads*, p. xxx, and 1534 in W. C. Hazlitt's *Handbook to the Popular Literature of Great Britain*, p. 228; but I have not seen this book. Another work of Gibson's is dated 1582 in Ritson's *Bibliographia Poetica*, p. 219, and in Charles Crawford's *Englands Parnassus*, p. xx. A Leonard Gibson, most probably our ballad-writer, was a student and chorister at New College, Oxford, in 1564–65 (Clark's *Register of Oxford*, II, ii, 22; Foster's *Alumni Oxoniensis*, Early Series, II, 562). It appears, then, very probable that Gibson had written No. 2 in time for its inclusion in the *Pleasant Sonnets* of 1566.

134. *Tantara.* Often *taratantara*, an echoic word describing the sound of a trumpet (occasionally the beating of a drum). George Puttenham (*Art of English Poesy*, 1589, ed. Arber, p. 192), defining *onomatopœia*, observes, "As the poet *Virgil* said of the sounding a trumpet, *ta-ra-tant, tara-tantara.*" Ballads called "A translated tantura of transetories present and terrors to come" and "the saylers newe tantara" were licensed on March 5, 1579, and July 19, 1584 (Arber, II, 348, 434). For ballads with a "tantara" refrain see Lilly's

Ballads, pp. 105, 292. Many other examples of the use of the word are cited in the *N. E. D.*, where a reference is also given to the famous verse of Ennius, "At tuba horribili sonitu taratantara dixit."

137. Supply the speaker's name, *Danea*.

153. After *ray* supply the refrain.

166. *Read* ¶ My.

171 f. The meaning seems to be: 'Methinks I hear your praise, methinks I hear (hear of) the race (course, or career) of your virtue.'

175. Supply *Danea*.

184. Supply *Diophon*.

No. 3, Line 196

The tune appears to be unknown.

In lines 267–270 the author bids farewell to Cambridge University in general and to "Gunuil Hall" in particular. Thanks to this passage, he can be unquestionably identified with the Thomas Richardson, aged eighteen, who was admitted pensioner to Gonville and Caius College on April 28, 1572 (*Biographical History of Gonville and Caius College*, ed. John Venn, I, 69). In all probability he was the "T. Richeson" whose name is signed to a ballad "To the toune of 'The raire & greatest gift'" (a tune named from the first line of a ballad that was registered on March 4, 1560, Arber, I, 127, and that is preserved in MS. Ashmole 48, ed. Wright, p. 44), found in MS. Cotton Vespasian A. XXV (ed. Boeddeker, II, 362). No. 3, then, was written in or after 1572, and of course was not in the 1566 *Pleasant Sonnets*.

The first reprint of this ballad was made by Thomas Evans, *Old Ballads*, I (1810), 59.

223. *hugie heape.* "The hugie heape of cares, that in this world I finde," — *Gorgeous Gallery*, p. 32.

235. *the Snake doth lie.* "In pleasant greene, doo stinging serpents lye," "I see the Serpent vile, that lurkes vnder the grene," — *Paradise*, pp. 29, 100; "I know vnder the

grene the serpent how he lurkes," — *Tottel's Miscellany*, ed. Arber, p. 6; "A poisoned serpent couered all with flowers," — William Byrd's *Psalmes, Sonets, & songs*, 1588, No. 25. The figure perhaps shows the influence of Virgil's "latet anguis in herba."

236. *ouergrowde. Read* ouergrown.

270. *Gunuil Hall.* See note to line 196, above.

No. 4, Line 287

The first line of this ballad, "Attend thee, go play thee," is used as the tune of a ballad called "The Louer exhorteth his Lady to bee constant," in the *Gorgeous Gallery*, 1578, p. 49 (cf. Chappell's *Popular Music*, I, 223). It is, therefore, self-evident that No. 4 is imitated by the *Gallery* ballad — not *vice versa* — and that it is at least earlier in date than 1578. The *Gallery* ballad begins as follows:

> Not light of loue lady,
> Though fancy doo prick thee,
> Let constancy possesse thy hart:
> Well worthy of blamyng:
> They bee, and defaming,
> From plighted troth which backe do start:
>   Deare dame:
> Then ficklenesse bannish,
> And folly extinguish,
> Bee skilfull in guiding,
>   And stay thee from slidinge
>   And stay thee. &c.

In the *Marriage of Wit and Wisdom*, 1579 (Shakespeare Society ed., p. 20), Wantonness sings a song "to the tune of 'Attend the goe playe the,'" probably suggested by the *Gallery* ballad, which was then new. No. 4 may well have been in the *Pleasant Sonnets* of 1566, although no date earlier than 1578 can be proved.

No. 4 is answered by the ballad next following (No. 5), and may also have been the work of "Peter Picks." The first three stanzas appear, with many verbal changes, in a

spurious MS. formerly owned by J. P. Collier (cf. the notes
to No. 15).

290. Proverbial. Cf. "Blest is the wooing thats not long
a dooing," — *Sir Giles Goosecap*, sig. F^v (*Tudor Facsimile
Texts*); "I like the wooing, that's not long a doing," —
King Leir (Hazlitt, *Shakespeare's Library*, II, ii, 328); "Blest
be the wooing speeds so soon of love," — *The Play of Stucley*
(Simpson, *The School of Shakspere*, I, 162); "Short wooing is
the best," — *The Two Angry Women of Abington*, sc. 13
(Gayley, *Representative English Comedies*, I, 620).

293. *silk and twist*. *Twist* is a noun meaning 'thread.'
That the phrase is correct as it stands, and that it is not, as
might be supposed, a misprint for *silken twist*, seems certain
from the appearance of *seame and silke* in line 304.

301. The line should be repeated as a refrain.

307. Proverbial. "Hot love soon cold" (Hazlitt's *English
Proverbs*, p. 217). Cf. "I see well hote love is soone colde," —
Lodge, *Rosalynd* (*Works*, ed. Hunterian Club, p. 91); "Itt
is told of old, soone hott, soone cold," — *The Nutbrown
Maid*, line 127 (*Percy Folio Manuscript*, ed. Hales and
Furnivall, III, 181); "This is hot love, that vanisheth like
vapours," — Fletcher, *The Maid in the Mill*, III, iii.

332. Proverbial. "The tide tarrieth no man" (Hazlitt's
English Proverbs, p. 400).

334. One line — perhaps *How then?* — was omitted by the
printer.

No. 5, Line 354

This ballad is in the same measure, and was probably
written by the same person, as No. 4. Peter Picks is no doubt
a pseudonym. No. 5 must be of about the same date as No. 4.

364. *better change*. That is, better exchange, meaning 'to
exchange me for a better man.'

377. *Goe too*. That is, *go to!* This should be a separate line
(like line 365), but the arrangement of the stanzas is confused
throughout.

380. Supply ¶.

387. Supply ¶.

399. *Nicibicetur* (or *nicebecetur*), a fanciful formation from *nice*, meaning a dainty (hard-to-please) person. The *N. E. D.* cites four or five instances of the word earlier than 1584.

No. 6, Line 403

The initials I. P. may possibly be those of John Pitt (or Pitts), a prolific writer of broadsides, who flourished *circa* 1560; but, as Pitt's extant work is all religious in character, the attribution to him of this secular ditty would seem to be of dubious validity. In 1571 Richard Jones, the printer of the *Handful*, published a broadside on "A meruaylous straunge deformed Swyne" (Lilly's *Ballads*, p. 186) that is signed by an I. P. who may have been the author of No. 6.

The title of the ballad means: "Dame Beauty's Reply to the Lover Who Wrote a Complaint Called 'Where is the life that late I led?'" No. 6 is, to repeat, a reply to a lost ballad that began — as the snatch sung by Petruchio in *The Taming of the Shrew*, IV, i, 143, evidences —

> Where is the life that late I led?
> Where are those. . . .

That the words of the second line omitted by Petruchio were "pleasant days" is indicated not only by the phrase, "pleasant to thine eies," in line 407 of the *Handful*, but also by Pistol's remark in *2 Henry IV*, V, iii, 147 f. (cf. Anders, *Shakespeare's Books*, p. 181):

> "Where is the life that late I led?" say they:
> Why, here it is; welcome these pleasant days!

This lost ballad was undoubtedly that registered by Richard Jones about March, 1566 (Arber, I, 308), as "a newe ballet of one who myslykeng his lybertie soughte his owne bondage through his owne folly." It may have been suggested by a ballad, beginning

> My frynd, the lyf I lead at all
> By thes fewe wordes perceave youe shall,

that had previously been registered (Arber, I, 306) and that is preserved in MS. Ashmole 48, ed. Wright, p. 38.

The facts just given furnish good evidence that No. 6 had appeared before the 1566 *Pleasant Sonnets* was compiled. That it had appeared before 1578 is certain, for it is imitated in the *Gorgeous Gallery* (p. 51) by a poem called "The Louer wounded with his Ladies beauty craueth mercy. To the Tune of *where is the life that late I led*." The priority of the *Handful* ballads to those contained in the *Gorgeous Gallery* is proved beyond cavil in my notes to Nos. 4, 18, 19, 23, and 27.

The tune is apparently unknown.

429. *the Gods of loue.* Possibly there is a faint reference here to William Elderton's extremely popular ballad of this title which is discussed in the introduction to No. 16.

435. The same idea is expressed in lines 233-234.

464. Possibly the *Gorgeous Gallery*, p. 47, borrows this line: "My minde that erst was free."

473. Supply ¶.

483. Proverbial (cf. 505). "Spare to speak and spare to speed" (Hazlitt's *English Proverbs*, p. 355). Cf. "Who spareth to speke, he spareth to spede,"—Lydgate, *Kalendare, Aprilis* (Herrig's *Archiv*, LXXX, 119); "Who spareth to speke he spareth to spede," — Hawes, *The Pastime of Pleasure*, ed. Wright, p. 74 (and cf. p. 91); "For he that spares to speake must spare to speed,"—Heywood, *The Faire Maide of the Exchange* (*Dramatic Works*, ed. Pearson, II, 12).

489. *For taking holde*, etc. This seems to mean, 'It is too late (thou tell'st) to avoid capture — to fly from being caught.' *For* is apparently used in the sense, once common, of 'to prevent.' Cf. "Child Waters" (Child, *English and Scottish Popular Ballads*, No. 63, A, stanza 28):

> Take her up in thine armes two,
> For filinge [i.e. defiling] of her feete.

No. 7, Line 511

Chappell gives the tune of *Green sleeves* in his *Popular Music*, I, 228, and remarks that it was written in the reign of Henry VIII. In No. 7, however, the tune is called new, and the name occurs in the Stationers' Registers (Arber, II, 376) for the first time on September 3, 1580, when Richard Jones registered "A newe northen [*sic*] Dittye of ye Ladye Greene Sleves,"—certainly, I think, the present ballad. Within a very short space the following ballads were registered: "ye Ladie Greene Sleeves answere to Donkyn hir frende" on September 3, 1580; "Greene Sleves moralised to the Scripture Declaringe the manifold benefites and blessinges of God bestowed on sinfull manne" on September 15, 1580; "Greene Sleves and Countenaunce in Countenaunce is Greene Sleves" on September 18, 1580; "a merry newe Northen songe of Greenesleves begynninge the boniest lasse in all the land" on December 14, 1580; "A Reprehension againste Greene Sleves by William Elderton" on February 13, 1581; and "Greene Sleves is worne awaie, Yellowe Sleeves Comme to decaie, Blacke Sleeves I holde in despite, But White Sleeves is my delighte," on August 24, 1581 (Arber, II, 376, 378, 384, 388, 400). It seems certain, then, that No. 7 was not in the *Pleasant Sonnets* of 1566 but was added to the 1584 *Handful*. In *The Merry Wives of Windsor* Shakespeare twice refers to this ballad (II, i, 64; V, v, 22). It was first reprinted in George Ellis's *Specimens of the Early English Poets*, 3d ed., II (1803), 394. Later, with important notes, it was reprinted in F. W. Fairholt's *Satirical Songs and Poems on Costume* (Percy Society, XXVII, 1849).

562. *grossie.* Dialectic for 'thickish,' 'luxuriant'; or perhaps a misprint for *grassie.*

579. *clothed all in green.* "Green indeed is the colour of lovers," — *Love's Labour's Lost*, I, ii, 90. "Knaves in Kendal green" were said to have assaulted Falstaff (*1 Henry IV*, II, iv, 246). In *Churchyard's Challenge* (1593) we read that "our fathers wore . . . kendall greene, in sommer for a

show." On the unluckiness of green see Child's *English and Scottish Popular Ballads*, II, 196 ff.

No. 8, Line 617

The tune of *Row well, ye mariners*, is given in Chappell's *Popular Music*, I, 112. A ballad of that title was licensed to William Pekering in 1565–66, and within a short time a half dozen or more answers or imitations were licensed (Arber, I, 305, 340, 342, 355, 360, 362, 401). It is reasonable to assume, therefore, that No. 8 was written in 1565–66, when the ballad and the tune of "Row Well" were at the height of their popularity.

618. *L.* The ordinary abbreviation for *Lady*.

645. *lookes.* Possibly a misprint for *hookes* (baits, snares) or for *bookes.* In support of the latter conjecture note *pen* (line 635) and *lore* (line 639).

646. *gleams.* Bright glances. Cf. *A Midsummer-Night's Dream*, V, i, 279: "For, by thy gracious, golden, glittering gleams."

667. Cf. "My teares run down like streames," — *Gorgeous Gallery*, p. 39.

671. *that froward is.* 'She that is disdainful or ungracious.'

690. *For why?* The phrase means *because* (cf. line 1011), and the question-mark is unnecessary.

No. 9, Line 698

This ballad was registered in 1565–66 (Arber, I, 313) by Alexander Lacy under the title of "the goddes Diana &c." The tune of the *Quarter braules* was derived from a lost "ballett intituled *the Cater bralles bothe Wytty and mery*" that Thomas Colwell registered in 1565–66 (Arber, I, 298), and is possibly one of the thirty or more "braules" preserved in J. P. N. Land's *Het Luitboeck van Thysius*, Amsterdam, 1889. See the discussion in the London *Times Literary Supplement* for January 19, 1922, p. 45. Cotgrave's *Dictionarie*,

1611, defines *bransle* as "a brawle, or daunce, wherein many (men, and women) holding by the hands sometimes in a ring, and otherwhiles at length, moue all together."

Under the title of "A new Sonnet shewing how the Goddess Diana transformed Acteon into the shape of a Hart. To a new tune," this ballad appears in the *Roxburghe Ballads*, II, 520, where the editor, Chappell, lists a number of other late seventeenth-century copies. The phrase, "to a new tune," means 'to its own tune,' or 'to the tune of *Diana and her darlings dear*' — the first line. In my *Old English Ballads* (1920), p. 164, I showed that the tunes of *Diana* and *O man in desperation* (part of the music for the latter tune seems to be noted in Add. MS. 38,599, fol. 133ᵛ) were probably identical, certainly interchangeable. In the London *Times Literary Supplement* for December 22, 1921, I pointed out also that a copy of the ballad, dating as early as 1624, is preserved in the Manchester Free Reference Library, and that this copy is to be sung "to the tune of *Rogero*." *Rogero* itself is a very old tune, the music for which is given in Chappell's *Popular Music*, I, 93. It seems to follow, then, that the tunes of *Diana*, *O man in desperation*, and *Rogero* could be interchanged at will. But as all the broadside copies have rearranged the metrical and stanza forms of No. 9, none of the tunes just mentioned can be identical with the *Quarter braules*.

Since No. 9 is fragmentary, and since no other ballad in this miscellany is known to exist in broadside form, the Manchester ballad, as the earliest broadside version of No. 9 extant, is here given from a copy furnished by the kindness of Mr. Geoffrey R. Axon, of the Manchester Free Reference Library. On the same sheet with this ballad is printed "A Lullaby" (see the *Roxburghe Ballads*, II, 525), at the end of which is the colophon, "London, Printed for I[ohn]. W[right]. dwelling in the Old-Bayly."

A new Sonnet, shewing how the Goddesse *Diana* transformed
Acteon into the Shape of a Hart.

To the tune of, *Rogero*.

1 DIana and her Darlings Deare
    went walking on a Day,
Throughout the Woods and waters clear,
    for their disport and play:
The leaves aloft were gay and green
    and pleasant to behold,
These Nymphs they walkt the Trees between,
    under the shadow cold

2 So long at last they found a place
    of springs and waters cleare,
A fairer Bath their never was
    found out this thousand yeare:
Wherein *Diana* daintily
    her selfe began to bathe,
And all her Virgins faire and pure
    themselves did wash and lave.

3 And as the Nymphs in water stood,
    Acteon passed by
As he came running through the Wood,
    on them he cast his eye,
And he behold their bodies bare,
    then presently that tide:
And as the Nymphs of him were ware,
    with voyce aloud they cry'd.

4 And clos'd *Diana* round about
    to hide her body small
Yet she was highest in that rout,
    and seene above them all.
And when *Diana* did perceive
    where *Acteon* did stand,
A furious look to him she gave,
    And took her Bow in hand;

5 And as she was about to shoot,
    Acteon began to run
To bide he thought it was no boot,
    his former sights were done:

And as he thought from her to escape,
    she brought it so to passe,
[Inc]ontinent [1] she chang'd his shape
    [ev]en [1] running as he was.

6 Each Goddesse took *Diana's* part
    Acteon to transforme
To make of him a huge wild Hart
    there they did all determe:
His skin that was so fine and faire,
    was made a tawnie red,
His Body overgrowne with haire,
    from foot unto the head;

7 And on his head great hornes were set,
    most monstrous to behold,
A huger Hart was never met,
    nor seen upon the Mould;
His eares, his eyes, his face full faire,
    transformed were full strange,
His hands for feet compelled were
    throughout the Wood to range.

8 Thus was he made a perfect Hart,
    and waxed fierce and grim,
His former shapes did cleane depart
    from every joynt and limb:
But still his memory did remaine,
    although he might not speake,
Nor yet among his friends complaine,
    his wofull mind to breake.

9 At length he thought for to repaire,
    home to his dwelling place;
Anon his Hounds of him were ware,
    and gan to try a pace:
Then *Acteon* was sore agast,
    his Hounds would him devoure,
And from them then he fled full fast,
    with all his might and power;

[1] Torn.

10 He spared neither Bush nor Brake,
    but ran through thick and thin,
Withall the swiftnesse he could make,
    in hope to save his skin:
Yet were his hounds so neare his tayle,
    and followed him so fast,
His running might not him availe,
    for all his speed and haste.

    The second part, to the same tune.

11 FOr why his Hounds would never lin,
    till him they overtook,
And then they rent and tore the skin,
    and all his body shook;
I am your Master *Acteon*
    then cry'd he to his Hounds,
And made to them most rufull moane,
    with shrill lamenting sounds.

12 I have been he that gave you food,
    wherein I did delight,
Wherefore suck not your masters bloud,
    his feiendship [*sic*] to requite:
But those Curres of a cursed kind,
    of him had no remorse
Although he was their dearest friend,
    they pul'd him downe by force.

13 There was no man to take his part,
    the story telleth plain:
Thus *Acteon* formed like a Hart,
    amongst the Dogs was slaine.
You Hunters all that range the Woods,
    although you rise up rath,
Beware you come not neer the Floods
    where Virgins use to bathe.

14 For if *Diana* you espy
    among her Darlings deare
Your former shape she shall disguise,
    and make you hornes to weare.

And so I now conclude my Song,
   having no more to alledge,
If *Acteon* had right or wrong,
   let all faire Virgins judge.

The subject of No. 9 comes, of course, from Ovid's *Meta-morphoses*, III, 138–252. It is used also in the *Gorgeous Gallery*, where one of the poems (p. 65) is called "The Louer wisheth himselfe an Harte in the Foreste, (as Acteon was) for his Ladyes sake." Allusions to the ballad of "Diana and her darlings dear" are too numerous to be mentioned here. See, for example, Richard Brome's *Damoiselle*, V, 1, and *The Jovial Crew*, III (*Dramatic Works*, Pearson's reprint, I, 455; III, 396).

720. *liuelie.* Warm and vigorous. "And I of lyuely breath, the last shall spend," — *Gorgeous Gallery*, p. 142.

No. 10, Line 758

This unfortunately fragmentary ballad was almost certainly in print before 1566. It is one of very many imitations of William Elderton's "The Pangs of Love and Lovers' Fits" (J. P. Collier's *Old Ballads*, p. 25, Percy Society, vol. I; Collmann's *Ballads*, No. 39), the first stanza of which runs thus:

> Was not good kyng Salamon
> Ravished in sondry wyse,
> With every livelie Paragon
> That glistered before his eyes?
> If this be true, as trewe it was,
>   Lady! lady!
> Why should not I serve you, alas,
>   My deare lady?

Elderton's ballad was registered for publication in 1558–59 (Arber, I, 96), and was perhaps the most popular ballad written during Queen Elizabeth's reign. Abundant proof of this popularity is given in my article on "William Elderton," *Studies in Philology*, XVII (1920), 201. No. 10 may be one of the imitations of "The Pangs" that were entered at Stationers' Hall in 1561–62 and 1564–65 (Arber, I, 181, 270).

The tune of Elderton's ballad is unknown but is usually called simply *King Solomon*.

The first part of the ballad evidently dealt with a version of the "love-juice story" Shakespeare has familiarized in *A Midsummer-Night's Dream*. The second part, summarized (indirectly, no doubt) from Ovid's *Metamorphoses*, III, 339–510, deals with the story of Narcissus. Echo is not mentioned.

760. *Lady Venus grace.* *Venus* is a genitive without ending. Other examples occur in lines 988, 1083, 1269, 1620, 1857.

766. *Ladies mercilesse.* That is, lady's mercilessness; though *Ladies* may be a misprint for *Ladie*, and *mercilesse* an adjective.

783. *he died.* Read she died.

816. *Did use themselves.* Practise (or habitually exercise) themselves.

835. *drinke their owne disease.* Figurative, as in Chaucer's *Troilus*, III, 1035, — "But goodly drinketh up al his distresse," — and the *Franklin's Tale*, line 214, — "Withouten coppe he drank al his penaunce." Cf. also "Thus dranke I all mine owne disease," — *Tottel's Miscellany*, ed. Arber, p. 147. There is a pun on *disease* (sickness) and *disease* (not at ease).

No. 11, Line 839

A careful reading of the first two stanzas (especially lines 841–2, 850–1, 856–7) shows beyond any reasonable doubt that No. 11 is the ballad of "a harte Declarynge his heavenes wyshyng that yt were knowen" which Richard Jones registered in 1565–66 (Arber, I, 297), several months before he registered the *Pleasant Sonnets*. I. [John?] Tomson (the author also of No. 13) is too common a name to be confidently identified. The tune is apparently not known, though it may have been connected with "the tune of Siselia" to which "the tru Reporte in the prayse of my mistres," a ballad registered in 1569–70 (Arber, I, 403), was to be sung.

840. *Pavin.* A pavan was a stately costume dance. The figures for it, says Thomas Park, are described in MS. Rawlinson Poet. 108.

876. *the storie saith.* The story in this case was Robert Henryson's *Testament of Creseyde*, which, since it was found in all the collected editions of Chaucer, was generally thought to be Chaucer's own work. See my article on "The Troilus-Cressida Story from Chaucer to Shakespeare," *Publications of the Modern Language Association of America*, XXXII (1917), 383–429. Cf. line 1274.

897. *Read* ¶ Therefore.

No. 12, Line 911

The tune of *The Painter* is apparently unknown: the identification proposed in Chappell's *Popular Music*, I, 161, is untenable. It took its name from a ballad of "ye paynter in his pryntyshod" that was registered by Alexander Lacy in 1565–66. Moralizations of "The Painter" were registered in 1566–67 and 1568 (Arber, I, 297, 331, 380). In John Pikering's *Horestes*, 1567 (A. Brandl's *Quellen des Weltlichen Dramas in England vor Shakespeare*, 1898, p. 517), one of the stage directions is: "Enter the Vyce, synginge this song to ye tune of 'the Paynter'." The Vice sings four stanzas, the first of which runs thus:

> Stand backe, ye slepinge iackes at home,
>   And let me go.
> You lye, syr knaue; am I a mome?
>   Why saye you so?
> Tout, tout, you dare not come in felde,
> For feare you shoulde the goste vp yelde.
> With blose he gose, the gunne shot flye,
> It feares, it seares, and their doth lye.

No. 12, then, could have been, and probably was, in the 1566 *Pleasant Sonnets*.

940. *Least flinging fancies*. 'Lest unruly (or inconstant) whims or caprice.'

No. 13, Line 957

"A boke intituled *Perymus and Thesbye*" was licensed to William Griffith in July, 1563 (Arber, I, 215), and a ballad on this story would naturally have followed the book. No. 13, then, could have been, and probably was, in the 1566 *Pleasant Sonnets*. The story itself was familiar through its appearance in Chaucer's *Legend of Good Women*. Later versions in Arthur Golding's translation of Ovid's *Metamorphoses*, IV, 55–166, in 1567, and "The History of Pyramus and Thisbie truely translated," a poem in the *Gorgeous Gallery*, pp. 127–147, made the story more popular still; so that there was considerable point to Shakespeare's burlesque in *A Midsummer-Night's Dream*. That Shakespeare did burlesque the ballad on the *Pyramus-Thisbe* song is the contention of Georg Hart in his *Pyramus- & Thisbe-Sage*, 1891, pp. 22–23. The metre, he shows, is the same.

On the tune see No. 2, above; on the author, No. 11, above.

988. *Minus*. That is, *Ninus'*. In *A Midsummer-Night's Dream*, III, i, 99, Flute calls him "Ninny."

995. *to viewd*. An odd perfect infinitive for *to 'a' viewed*.

No. 14, Line 1050

The tune, which is given in Chappell's *Popular Music*, II, 793 (cf. also Malone's Variorum *Shakspeare*, XVII, 424–426), comes from the title of a ballad, "Callin o custure me," that was "tolerated" to John Allde on March 10, 1582 (Arber, II, 407). Accordingly, No. 14 cannot have been in the 1566 *Pleasant Sonnets*.

"Calen o Custure me" (as line 1051 has it) is supposed to be a corruption of "Cailín óg a stór" (meaning "Young girl, O treasure"), a popular Irish song. In *Henry V*, IV, iv, 4, Shakespeare makes Pistol address a Frenchman thus: "Qualtitie calmie custure me! Art thou a gentleman?" —

an obvious allusion to the original Irish ballad on which No. 14 was modelled (cf. Anders, *Shakespeare's Books*, pp. 169 f., 268) or, perhaps, to No. 14 itself.

No. 14 was first reprinted in Evans's *Old Ballads*, I (1810), 119.

1079 f. 'Although the looks of my love are flames that burn me (with unrequited passion), yet I wish I were nearer to the flames.'

1090. Unintelligible.

No. 15, Line 1096

William Griffith registered a ballad called "mayde Will you mary moralyzed" in 1570–71 (Arber, I, 437). This entry perhaps indicates that No. 15, the original ballad, was printed at a date nearer to 1570 than to 1566, although, of course, the entry may have been merely a reissue of the moralization.

The Black almain is the tune of a ballad by Stephen Peele (Collmann's *Ballads*, No. 65). "Almains" (dances, or dance-music in slow time, now called *Allemandes*) were very common (cf. No. 31, below). In John Phillip's comedy of *Patient Grissell*, 1566, sig. E ii, the Marquis sings a ballad "to the tune of the latter Almain." In Anthony Munday's *Banquet of Dainty Conceits*, 1588 (*Harleian Miscellany*, ed. Park, vol. IX), there are ballads to the tunes of the *Masker's Allemaigne, commonly called the Olde Allemaigne*, the *Venetian Allemaigne*, *Allemaigne Measure*, the *Scottish Allemaigne*, and *Mounsieures Allemaigne*.

Three stanzas of the ballad, all slightly changed, are reprinted from a spurious MS. in Collier's *Extracts*, II, 6–7. On this MS. see my note in the *Journal of English and Germanic Philology*, XVIII (1919), 53; the *Academy*, IX, 313, XXVII, 170; and *Notes and Queries*, 8th S., VII, 386.

1099, 1101. *to wed a, maidenhed a.* In his *Discourse of English Poetry* (1586) William Webbe sneered at "ryming Ballet makers and compylers of sencelesse sonets" who can "perhappes obserue iust number of sillables, eyght in one line, sixe in an other, and there withall an A to make a iercke in the ende."

1110. *be.* Read *do* for the sake of rhyme.

1127. Proverbial. "We have fished fair, and caught a frog" (Hazlitt's *English Proverbs*, p. 467). Cf. Chaucer's *Troilus*, II, 328: "than have ye fisshed faire." See further Heywood's *Woorkes*, 1562, Spenser Society ed., p. 26; *The Firste Parte of Churchyardes Chippes*, 1575, Collier's reprint, p. 33; Rollins, *A Pepysian Garland*, p. 318.

1131 f. 'Guarding you and hindering you from reassuming your natural (wanton) manner (as Argus watched and hindered the heifer Io).'

1134 f. Proverbial. "Though the cat winks a while, yet sure she is not blind" (Hazlitt's *English Proverbs*, p. 416). Cf. Rowlands, *A Crew of Kind Gossips*, Hunterian Club, p. 20: "The Cat oft winkes, and yet she is not blinde." See line 1496.

1146. *trap.* Read *traps* for the sake of rhyme.

1160. *from that I haue said.* "From that that (or which) I haue said" would suit the metre better.

1168. *leek you.* Like (love) for yourself.

No. 16, Line 1170

This is a moralization of William Elderton's famous ballad, "The Gods of Love" (cf. Collmann's *Ballads*, No. 7), which was printed in 1562, but which survives only in the snatch sung by Benedick in *Much Ado*, V, ii, 26:

> The god of love,
> That sits above,
> And knows me, and knows me,
> How pitiful I deserve.

See the discussion in my "William Elderton," *Studies in Philology*, XVII, 203 ff. Very many imitations and moralizations of Elderton's ballad were printed before 1566, and

it is altogether probable that No. 16 was in print by that
date.

1178. *Paul.* See 1 Corinthians, vii. Cf. Burton's *Anatomy
of Melancholy* (1638 ed., p. 566): "Marriage replenisheth the
earth, but virginity Paradise, *Elias*, *Eliseus*, *Iohn Baptist*
were Bacchelours, virginity is a pretious Iewell, a faire gar-
land, a never fading flowre, for why was *Daphne* turned to a
green Bay tree, but to shew that virginity is immortall?"
See also John Phillip, *Patient Grissell*, 1566, sig. B iii.

1207. The question-mark should be a period.

1212 f. 'But it is hard to find a hundred in twenty — and
just so hard is it to find a chaste woman.'

No. 17, Line 1214

Richard Jones registered this as "a ballett intituled *ye
lovynge Wormes comme learne of me,*" in July, 1565 (Arber, I,
293). Not knowing that fact, R. W. Bond reprinted the
ballad — which contains an extraordinary number of wise
saws and proverbs — among the early poems of John Lyly
(*Works*, III, 465), and in marginal glosses called attention
to resemblances between the ideas and phraseology of the
ballad and Lyly's acknowledged work. Bond (p. 438) de-
clares that "few, I believe, will be found to question the
correctness of my attribution of . . . *A Warning for Wooers*"
to Lyly. As Lyly was a mere lad when No. 17 was first
printed, the attribution cannot, of course, be considered.
"You loving Wormes that linked be in Cupid's clogging
chain" is the beginning of "A Lover bewailing the Absence
of his Love. To the tune of, *Where is the Life of late?*" in *The
Garland of Delight*, 1681, Song XXVIII.

In his *Memoranda on Love's Labour's Lost*, p. 70, Halliwell-
Phillipps says that the name of Shakespeare's comedy, *Love's
Labour's Lost*, may have been suggested by lines in our
ballad.

The tune is not known to me. The only ballad title that
resembles it is "Sutle Simon or Simon the Sutle of Salisbury

plaine," but this was a late ballad, registered on December 19, 1637 (Arber, IV, 402).

Five stanzas of No. 17 were reprinted in George Ellis's *Specimens of the Early English Poets*, 3d ed., II (1803), 399; seven stanzas in *Censura Literaria*, VI (1808), 259–261.

To the same measure and in the same proverbial phraseology as No. 17 was written "a ballett intituled of *lyngerynge Love*" that was registered by William Griffith in 1563–64 (Arber, I, 238), and that is preserved in MS. Cotton Vespasian A. XXV (ed. Boeddeker, II, 211) and in MS. Rawlinson Poet. 148. From the latter manuscript Bond (p. 463) has printed the ballad, which, like No. 17, he wrongly attributes to Lyly. The first stanza runs thus:

> In lingeringe Loue mislikinge growes,
> Wherby our fancies ebbs and flowes:
> We love to day, and hate to morne,
> And dayly wher we list to scorne.
>   Take heede therfore,
>   If she mislike, then love no more:
>   Quicke speed makes waste,
> Loue is not gotten in such haste.

1232. Cf. Hoffmann von Fallersleben, Tunicius's *Niederdeutsche Sprichwörtersammlung*, p. 99, No. 1234: "Arstedye kumt to late als de kêrl dôt is. Vita defuncto sero medicamina fiunt." Also Chaucer's *Troilus*, V, 741–742:

> But al to late cometh the letuarie
> Whan men the cors un-to the grave carie.

1234. Cf. Chaucer's *Troilus*, III, 855–861.

1237. Cf. "Whan the grete Stiede Is stole, thanne he taketh hiede, And makth the stable dore fast," — Gower, *Confessio Amantis*, IV, 901–903; "Whan the stede is stolyn to shyt the stable dore," — Barclay, *The Ship of Fools*, ed. Jamieson, I, 76; "But I, alas! when steede is stolin, Doo shut the stable dore," — *Marriage of Wit and Wisdom*, ed. Halliwell, p. 55; "Quant en a le cheval perdu A tart va l'en fermer l'estable," — *Roman de Galerent*, lines 1453–1454;

"To late . . . is . . . Whan the stéede is stolne shut the stable durre," — John Heywood's *Woorkes* (1562), Spenser Society ed., p. 21. See also Richard Hill's *Songs* (*ca.* 1536), ed. R. Dyboski, 1907, p. 128, and George Turbervile's *Tragical Tales* (*ca.* 1574), 1837 reprint, p. 282.

1240. Proverbial. "Had I wist was a fool" (Hazlitt's *English Proverbs*, p. 160). A poem in the *Paradise*, p. 13, is entitled "Beware of had I wyst." Cf. "Beth wele war before, and thenk of *had I wyst*," — *Archæologia*, XXIX, 341; "Be war of haddywyst," — *Reliquiæ Antiquæ* I, 74, 77; "Thus fulofte hirself sche skiereth And is al war of 'hadde I wist,'" — Gower, *Confessio Amantis*, II, 472–473; "And lok thou thynk of had-i-wyst,"—Wright, *Songs and Carols*, Percy Society, p. 24; "Thanne is to late to sey, if I had wiste," — anon., in Lydgate's *Minor Poems*, ed. Halliwell, p. 28; "Than may we synge of had y wist," — *Hymns to the Virgin*, ed. Furnivall, p. 80; "Most miserable man, whom wicked fate Hath brought to court to sue for had-y-wist, That few have found, and manie one hath mist!"— Spenser, *Mother Hubberds Tale*, lines 892–894; "Had I wist is a great fault," — Greene, ed. Grosart, VIII, 125; "Had I wist doth seldome serue as a blasone of good vnderstanding," — Gascoigne's *Posies*, 1575 (*Works*, ed. Hazlitt, I, 15).

1241. See Hazlitt, *English Proverbs*, p. 150; John Heywood, *Woorkes*, 1562, Spenser Society ed., pp. 7, 169; Thomas Mowntayne in J. G. Nichols, *Narratives of the Reformation*, p. 205. This proverb occurs also in the *Merchant of Venice*, II, v, 54; in *Les Proverbes del Vilain*; and in Tusser's *Five Hundred Points of Good Husbandry* ("Washing").

1243. *times*. *Read* tunes.

1248. 'By means of Cupid's snares you shall overthrow him.'

1255. Proverbial. "Look ere you leap" (Hazlitt's *English Proverbs*, p. 279). Jasper Heywood has a poem called "Looke or you leape" in the *Paradise*, p. 134. Cf. "to loke afore we light," — *Tottel's Miscellany*, ed. Arber, p. 216.

1263. *rule the roste* (roast). To be master. Cf. *2 Henry VI*, I, i, 109.

1266. Proverbial: "Experto crede." Cf. Hazlitt's *English Proverbs*, p. 459, "Try the ice before you venture upon it;" "Trye before you trust," — *Paradise*, p. 38; "Be constant to them that trust thee, & trust them that thou hast tried,"—Lyly's *Euphues and His England* (*Works*, ed. Bond, II, 149).

1269. 'Instead of the skill of Pallas and the strength of Juno he chose that which bred,' etc.

1275. *Romeus*. A book called *The Tragicall history of the Romeus and Juliett with sonettes* was registered in 1562–63 (Arber, I, 203). This was by Arthur Brooke; Richard Tottel printed it, and reprinted it in 1582. No ballad seems to have been written on this story until August 5, 1596 (Arber, III, 68), and for that ballad Shakespeare's tragedy was without doubt the source.

1276. *Piramus*. See No. 13, line 957.

1277. *Iphis*. Ovid, *Metamorphoses*, XIV, 698. The first ballad on this subject seems to have been printed in 1569–70 (Arber, I, 403): "the vnfortunate ende of Iphis sonne vnto Teucer kynge of Troye." "The Pangs of Love" (cf. No. 10, above) shows that Elderton knew the story in 1559; it is referred to also in the *Gorgeous Gallery*, p. 104. Later Thomas Nashe (*Works*, ed. McKerrow, III, 67) spoke of "The storie of Axerex [Anaxarete] and the worthie Iphijs." Iphis and Hercules are twice linked together in Lyly's *Works* (ed. Bond, III, 567).

1278. *ridden be like Hercules*. A famous tale of Aristotle — Oriental in origin — tells how that philosopher was so besotted with love that to please his sweetheart he allowed her, much to the amusement of his pupil Alexander, to bridle him, got down on all fours, and was ridden by her. See Henri d'Andeli's *Lai d'Aristote;* the Middle High German *Aristoteles und Phillis*, ed. J. L. Campion, *Modern Philology*, XIII, 347 ff.; A. Borgeld, *Aristoteles en Phyllis*

(1902); Ward, *Catalogue of Romances*, III, 87; A. Wessel-
ski, *Mönchslatein* (1909), No. 128, pp. 167, 244–251. I ac-
cept Professor Kittredge's suggestion that the ballad-writer
has inadvertently transferred this story to Hercules, who
made himself ridiculous with Omphale, permitting her to
carry his club and wear his lion's skin, while he (dressed in
her clothes) plied the distaff. According to Lucian, Omphale
even chastised him with her slipper, as if he had been a female
slave. Mr. Kittredge refers me to a fifteenth-century collec-
tion of Spanish poems, *El Cancionero de Juan Alfonso de
Baena*, in which a poem (No. 533) ascribed to Ferrant San-
chez Calavera transfers the story of Aristotle's being ridden
to Hercules. He refers me also to Borgeld's *Aristoteles en
Phyllis*, pp. 16–17, where the transference of the story from
Aristotle to Virgil is discussed; and points out numerous
references in English works which prove that the Aristotle
story was well known in England before the date of the pres-
ent ballad. — A ballad called "Herculis and his ende" was
registered in 1563–64 (Arber, I, 236). What appears to be
a line from it or a similar ballad is sung in Chapman's *May-
Day*, IV, i.

1281. *Midas.* A ballad called "the mesyrable state of
kynge Medas" was registered in 1569–70 (Arber, I, 401).

1289. *Of grasse commeth hay.* Proverbial. "Such men as
you are Gentleman, who thinke greene grasse will neuer be
drye Hay," — Lyly's *Euphues and His England* (*Works*, ed.
Bond, II, 134).

1291. Proverbial. "Soon ripe, soon rotten" (Hazlitt's
English Proverbs, p. 354). "Timely ripe is rotten too too
soone," — Greene, *Frier Bacon and Frier Bongay*, II, iii, 701
(ed. Collins, II, 37); "The proverbe olde is verified, soon
ripe and soon rotten," — Preston, *King Cambises* (ed. Haw-
kins, I, 291).

1295. *Read* ¶ Some.

1298. *common folke vse common sport.* Perhaps this was
the *motif* of the ballad called "The daylie exercise of ye comen

sort of men" that Edward Allde registered on August 1, 1586 (Arber, II, 450).

1299 f. Proverbial. "Sundry men are of sundry mindes, one looketh high as one y^t feareth no chips," — Lyly's *Euphues and His England* (*Works*, ed. Bond, II, 219); "For who so heweth ouer hye, The chippes wyll fall in his eye," — Hazlitt, *Remains of the Early Popular Poetry*, III, 177; "Hewe not to hye, lest the chips fall in thine iye," — Heywood's *Woorkes* (1562), Spenser Society ed., p. 67. See also Gower, *Confessio Amantis*, I, 1917 f., and Richard Hill's *Songs* (*ca.* 1536), ed. R. Dyboski, 1907, p. 129.

1310. *venom . . . tode.* Cf. *As You Like It*, II, i, 13, "like the toad, ugly and venomous."

No. 18, Line 1319

The tune derives its name from "a ballett intituled *All in a garden grene/ betwene ij lovers*" that was registered by William Pekering in 1565 and, under a briefer title, by William Griffith in 1568–69 (Arber, I, 295, 388). A ballad written to fit these entries occurs in Collier's spurious MS. (cf. No. 15, above), and is reprinted in his *Extracts*, I, 196. The genuine ballad, however, appears under the title, "A merrye new ballad, of a countrye wench and a clowne. To a fine tune," in Andrew Clark's *Shirburn Ballads*, 1907, p. 220. It begins:

> All in a garden greene,
>   where late I layde me downe
> Vppon a banke of camemeyle,
>   where I sawe vpon a style,
>   sitting, a countrey Clowne.

Each stanza has twenty-eight lines. Obviously the septenaries of No. 18 could not have been sung to the "fine tune" of this "All in a Garden Green." There must have been two tunes of this name, unless its use for No. 18 was due to an error on the part of the printer. The music given by Chappell, *Popular Music*, I, 110, for *All in a garden green* does not fit the Shirburn ballad but can have been used for No. 18.

The first two stanzas of No. 18 were copied verbatim in MS. Ashmole 48, ed. Wright, p. 183, — convincing proof (cf. the introductory notes to No. 2) that the ballad had appeared in print before the 1566 *Pleasant Sonnets* was compiled. They run as follows:

> My fancie did I fix
>   In faithfull forme and frame,
> In hope there should no bloustringe blast
>   Have power to move the same;
> And as the godes do knowe and world can witnesse bere,
> I never served other saynt nor idole other where.

Since the date of *circa* 1566 is established for No. 18, it is certain that the ballad called "The Louer complayneth of his Ladies vnconstancy" in the *Gorgeous Gallery*, pp. 47 f., is a plagiarism of it, not *vice versa* (cf. the introductory notes to Nos. 4, 6, 19, 23, 27). With lines 1327–30, 1335–38, 1365–80, and 1391–94 compare the following stanzas from the *Gorgeous Gallery*:

[9]
And fixt on Fancyes lore,
   As world can witnesse beare,
No other saynct I did adore;
   Or Idole any whear

[10]
Ne will, no wo, or smart
   Could minde from purpose fet,
But that I had a Iasons harte
   The golden fleese to get.

[11]
Ne for my part I swere
   By all the Gods aboue,
I neuer thought on other fere
   Or sought for other loue.

[12]
In her the like consente
I saw ful oft appear,
If eyes be iudge of that is mente
Or eares haue power to heare.

[13]
Yet woordes be turnd to winde
A new found gest hath got
The Fort, which once, to vndermine
And win I planted shot.

[14]
Her freend that ment her well
Out of conceyt is quite,
While others beares away yᵉ bell
By hitting of the white.

[15]
In this our wauering age
So light are womens mindes,
As Aspen leafe yᵗ stil doth rage
Though aeole calme his windes.

1343. *Read* ¶ With.

1355. *Read* ¶ True.

1373. Proverbial. "Words are but wind, but blows un-
kind" (Hazlitt's *English Proverbs*, p. 499). Cf. "Wordes are
but wynde,"—Wager, *Marie Magdalene*, ed. Carpenter, p. 75.

1377. *Read* ¶ Her.

1381. *Read* ¶ He. *Beat the bush.* The *N. E. D.* gives many
examples of this proverb, as "Many a man doth bete the bow,
Another man hath the brydde," from the *Coventry Mysteries*
(1400).

1385. Park suggests a reference to the game of hopscotch,
but more probably a dance is referred to. Cf. Chaucer's
Troilus, II, 1106 f.:

"How ferforth be ye put in loves daunce?"
"By god," quod he, "I hoppe alwey bihinde!"

See also Heywood's *Woorkes*, 1562, Spenser Society ed., p. 7.

No. 19, Line 1425

The tune of *Raging love* indicates that this ballad had appeared in print before 1566. It takes its name from the first line, "When ragyng loue with extreme payne," of Lord Surrey's poem, "The louer comforteth himself with the worthinesse of his loue," in *Tottel's Miscellany*, ed. Arber, p. 14. Surrey's poem had been registered for publication as a broadside ballad in 1557, 1560–61, and 1561–62 (Arber, I, 75, 154, 177). It was also imitated by W. F.'s [William Fulwood's?] "A new Ballad against Unthrifts" — beginning "When raging louts, with feble braines" — that was registered in 1561–62 (Lilly's *Ballads*, p. 153; Arber, I, 180). Like Nos. 4, 6, 18, 23, and 27, the present ballad was unblushingly plagiarized in the *Gorgeous Gallery*. "The Louer complayneth" (p. 47), for example, borrows from lines 1447–50 in the following fashion:

[17]

What paps did giue them food
That weue sutch webs of wo
What beast is of so cruell mood
That countes his freend for fo.

More striking still is the plagiarism in "The Louer wounded with his Ladies beauty craueth mercy," pp. 51–52. Compare, for example, lines 1451–68 with the following stanzas:

[3]

Like as the tender turtle Doue
Doth wayle the losse of mate,
In mourning weed, so spend I tyme
Lamentinge mine estate.
The night renewes my cares
When weary limmes would rest,
And dreadfull dreames abandon sleepe
Which had my greefes represt.
I drench my couch with teares
Which flow from gushing eyes,
A thousand heapes of hidden thoughtes
In minde I doo deuise.

[4]

Full often times it dooth mee good
　　To haunt and vew the place,
Where I receiued my wound, alas
　　By vewing of thy face.
Full oft it ioyes my hart
　　To kisse that clot of clay
From whence thou shot those louing lookes
　　Which bred my whole decay.
O blessed place I cry
　　Though woorker of my payne,
Render I craue most hartely
　　To mee my loue agayne.

The *Handful* ballad is, furthermore, frankly imitated by
George Whetstone in "The complaint of a gentlewoman,
being with child, falsely forsaken," a poem in his *Rocke of
Regard*, 1576 (Collier's reprint, p. 127). With lines 1425 ff.
compare Whetstone's second stanza:

　　Though reason would I should refraine
　　His blame, my shame for to bewray,
　　Good ladies, yet my pinching paine
　　Injoynes mee here the truth to say,
　　Whose wretched plight and pensive state
　　Surmounteth farre Queene Didoes fate.

No. 19 is answered by No. 20.

1433 f. These lines are repeated in lines 1483 f.

1436. *stormes.* Apparently a misprint for *scornes.*

1481. *to my pay.* 'As a reward for love I have only
deceit.'

1483 f. *here and after.* Identical in meaning with lines
1433 f.

No. 20, Line 1487

No evidence for dating this ballad can be found except
that it appears to be an answer to No. 19 and, in that case,
probably followed it immediately. R. W. Bond, "with some
doubts," attributes the authorship of No. 20 to John Lyly

(*Works*, III, 440, 468). But he is not convincing (cf. the notes to No. 17, above).

Seven stanzas of No. 20 were reprinted in *Censura Literaria*, VI (1808), 258–259.

1489. Omit the comma after *deuise* and the meaning of the line becomes obvious.

1496. Proverbial. Cf. line 1134 n.

1511. *seemst to dim my sight.* Mr. Kittredge explains this as "one of the old (and rather baffling) uses of *seem* — which survives in the colloquial 'I can't seem to think,' 'I can't seem to do it.' The idea, approximately, is: 'In vain you try to dim'; or, more literally, 'you give yourself the appearance of dimming.'"

1512. Rowling (rolling) eyes were sometimes thought to be a sign of wantonness.

1530. *Belles.* The figure comes from falconry.

No. 21, Line 1531

No evidence for the date of this ballad can be found.

The tune, *Kypascie*, derives its name from a dance, properly called *Qui passa*. William Elderton's "A proper newe Ballad sheweing that philosophers learnynges are full of good warnynges" (Lilly's *Ballads*, p. 139), which was registered in 1568 (Arber, I, 384), was "songe to the tune of my Lorde Marques Galyarde, or the firste traces of Que passa." It has, however, a measure different from that of No. 21.

No. 22, Line 1568

This ballad was in the edition to which the single leaf reprinted on pp. 73–75, above, belonged. If this leaf came from an edition earlier than that of 1584 (and that it did so seems to me certain), then the date of No. 22 is established. Otherwise, I find nothing to assist in dating it. The tune is unknown.

1578. *Palemon.* This reference (cf. also line 1619) to the

Knight's Tale is only another instance of the popularity of Chaucer.

1584 f. Cf. the *Æneid*, IV, 365–367:

> Nec tibi diva parens, generis nec Dardanus auctor,
> Perfide, sed duris genuit te cautibus horrens
> Caucasus, Hyrcanaeque admorunt ubera tigres.

1589. *rent.* Rend. "The Bibles they did rent and teare," — Lilly's *Ballads*, p. 267; "And will you rent our ancient love asunder?" — *A Midsummer-Night's Dream*, III, ii, 215.

No. 23, Line 1602

The tune of *Apelles* indicates that No. 23 had appeared before 1566. It is used for a song in Barnabe Googe's *Epitaphes*, 1563, and ballads to the tune were registered in 1565–66 (Arber, I, 298, 312). A later ballad (1569) to the same tune is in Lilly's *Ballads*, p. 56. That No. 23 had certainly appeared before 1578 is proved by the fact that a ballad in the *Gorgeous Gallery* borrows its title and most of its lines. The *Gallery* ballad (pp. 51 f.) runs thus:

> [2]
> In viewing thee I tooke sutch ioy
>   As wofull wight in rest
> Vntill the blinded boy I felte
>   Assault my captiue brest.
> And since that time alas
>   Such pinching payne I taste
> That I am now remedilesse
>   If mercy make not haste.
> For hid in deepe dispayre
>   My teares are all my ioy,
> I burne, I freese, I sinke, I swim
>   My wealth is mine annoy.

> [5]
> Not wofull Monsier dom Dieg
>   Or Priams noble sonne,
> Constrayned by loue did euer mone
>   As I for thee haue donne.

Sir Romeus annoy
  But trifle seemes to mine,
Whose hap in winning of his loue
  Did clue of cares vntwine.
My sorrowes haue no ende
  My hap no ioy can spie,
The flowing Fountayne of my teares
  Beginneth to waxe drie.

[6]

Let pitty then requyte my payne
  O woorker of my woe,
Let mercy milde possesse thy harte
  Which art my freendly foe.
Receiue the hart which heare
  I yeeld into her hand,
Which made by force a breach in Fort
  Which I could not withstande.
Thou hast in Ballance paysd
  My life and eke my death,
Thy loyalty contaynes my ioy.
  Disdayne will stop my breath.

[7]

If constant loue may reape his hire
  And fayth may haue his due,
Good hope I haue your gentill hart
  My grislie greefe will rue.
And that at length I shall
  My hartes delight imbrace:
When due desart by curtesie,
  Shall purchase mee thy grace.
Vntill which time, my deare
  Shall still increase my payne,
In pensiue thoughtes and heauinesse
  Because I shall remayne.

No. 23 was probably suggested by Sir Thomas Wyatt's poem, beginning "The liuely sparkes, that issue from those eyes," in *Tottel's Miscellany*, ed. Arber, p. 34.

1620. *Pyramus*. A mistake for *Pryamus* (*Priam*). Contrariwise, the spelling *Priamus* for *Piramus* occurs in Elderton's "Pangs of Love" (a ballad referred to in the introductory note to No. 10).

No. 24, Line 1631

From the tune it is obvious that this ballad could have been in the 1566 *Pleasant Sonnets*. To this tune was sung "A Newe Ballade of a Lover," licensed in 1563 (Lilly's *Ballads*, pp. 24, 278; Arber, I, 204). In John Phillip's *Patient Grissell*, 1566, sig. C 4, "Here Grissell Singith a songe, to the tune of Damon & Pithias." "A ballett intituled *tow* [sic] *lamentable songes Pithias and Damon*" was licensed in 1565–66 (Arber, I, 304). A song (evidently to this tune) on Damon and Pythias occurs in Richard Edwards's play of *Damon and Pythias*, 1564 (Dodsley-Hazlitt's *Old Plays*, IV, 43).

1641. *I waile oft times in woe.* This line, which seems to be imitated by line 1917, was itself most probably borrowed from the ballad called "the Crueltye of fortayne/ [beginning] I weepe for Woo and I Dye for payne" that Richard Hudson registered in 1565–66 (Arber, I, 293).

1653. *Susanna.* The story of Susanna and the Elders was the subject of a ballad registered in 1562–63 (Arber, I, 210). The ballad itself was enormously popular — Sir Toby Belch quotes the first line of it in *Twelfth Night* — and has survived in numerous, though rather late, copies (see the *Roxburghe Ballads*, I, 190).

1654. *Pancalier.* Accused of adultery by the Earl of Pancalier, the Duchess of Savoy (the King of England's sister) was delivered "by the prowesse and valiaunt combate of Don John di Mendozza, (a gentleman of Spaine)." The reference here undoubtedly came from Thomas de la Peend's metrical story of *The History of John Lord Mandozze*, 1565 (see *The British Bibliographer*, II, 523), or from William Painter's *Palace of Pleasure*, 1566, Book I, Novel 45. The story of the Duchess of Savoy had earlier been told by Boaistuau, Bandello, and Belleforest.

No. 25, Line 1672

This ballad was certainly in print by 1566.

In MS. Ashmole 48, ed. Wright, p. 195, there is a ballad
on Troilus and Cressida "To the tune of Fayne woold I fynd
sum pretty thynge to geeve unto my lady" — a tune named
from No. 25 — that was registered in 1565–66 (Arber, I,
300). Moralizations of No. 25, entitled "a fayne wolde I
have a godly thynge to shewe vnto my ladye" and "fayne
wolde I have a vertuous wyfe adourned with all modeste
bothe mylde and meke of quyett lyf esteemynge chef hyr
chastetye," were licensed in 1566–67 (Arber, I, 340, 342).
Probably in imitation of No. 25, also, was written the ballad
of "fayne would I haue and take no payne" that was regis-
tered on October 1, 1576 (Arber, II, 303).

The first reprint of this ballad was that in Thomas Evans's
Old Ballads, I (1810), 122. The music of *Lusty gallant*
is given in Chappell's *Popular Music*, I, 91.

A second copy of No. 25 is preserved in MS. Rawlinson
Poet. 108, fol. 44, whence it is reprinted in my *Old English
Ballads*, 1920, pp. 322–324. It has no title, is two stanzas
(lines 1695–98, 1707–12) shorter than the printed version,
and is of about the same date as the 1584 *Handful of Pleasant
Delights*.

1679. The MS. has "I meane no hurt, I meane no harme."

1692. *gases.* That is, gazes = steady looks or "gapings."
The latter is the word used in the MS.

1693. *gaping.* The MS. has *wandringe.*

No. 26, Line 1725

There is no evidence for dating this ballad. Possibly it
was suggested by No. 15, above, or by Sir Thomas Wyatt's
poem called "To a ladie to answere directly with yea or nay"
(*Tottel's Miscellany*, ed. Arber, p. 41). The tune is apparently
unknown.

1744. *you Louer. Read* your Louer.
1775. *Now. Read* ¶ Now.

No. 27, Line 1781

The tune of *I loved her over well* (which is used also for No.
32, below) probably (as lines 1779, 1808, and 1825 show)
derived its name from this ballad itself. It is pretty good
evidence that No. 27 was in the 1566 *Pleasant Sonnets*.
What seems to have been a reply to No. 27, a ballad called
"a ffayrewell to Alas I lover [*sic*] you over well &c," was
registered by William Griffith in 1567–68 (Arber, I, 362).
No. 27 is imitated by passages in the *Gorgeous Gallery*, p. 39,
and accordingly was certainly in print before 1578. With
lines 1810–17 and line 1819 compare these stanzas:

[10]
The wretched hound that spends his dayes,
    And serveth after kinde:
The Horse that treadeth ye beaten ways
    As nature doth him binde

[11]
In age yet findes releefe,
    Of them that did him wo:
Who in their great mischeefe,
    Disdayne not them to know.

It may be worth adding that a poem purporting to have been
written by John Harington to Isabella Markham in 1594
(*Nugae Antiquae*, ed. Park, II, 326) begins:

Alas! I love you overwell,
Myne owne sweete deere delygte!

1810. *Read* ¶ The hound.

No. 28, Line 1844

The tune of *Rogero* is given in Chappell's *Popular Music*, I,
93, but *New Rogero* seems to be unknown. To the latter
tune were sung William Elderton's "Lamentation of Follie,"

which was printed after February 15, 1584 (Collmann's *Ballads*, No. 43; Collier's *Old Ballads*, p. 45, Percy Society, vol. I); and Arthur Bourcher's "A worthy Mirrour," dated 1589 (Collmann's *Ballads*, No. 10; Collier's *Old Ballads*, p. 92; *Roxburghe Ballads*, III, 87). From these facts it seems reasonable to suppose that No. 28 was added to the 1584 edition of the *Handful*.

No. 29, Line 1914

This ballad was not in the 1566 *Pleasant Sonnets*. It was registered by Richard Jones on November 7, 1576 (Arber, II, 304), as "A woefull ballade made by master George Mannyngton an houre before he suffered at Cambridge castell 1576." From a manuscript source it was printed in the *Gentleman's Magazine* for January, 1781 (LI, 36–37), whence it was reprinted in Joseph Ritson's *Ancient Songs from the Time of King Henry the Third to the Revolution*, 1792, pp. 150 ff. The chief variations between Ritson's reprint and the *Handful* version are given in the notes below.

No other ballad in the *Handful* was so popular as No. 29; none is more frequently alluded to. It was regarded as a "good-night," or last farewell, *par excellence*. The farewell addresses in lines 1949, 1959, and 1981 served as models for many other ballad-writers. Samuel Rowlands, in his *Melancholie Knight*, 1615 (*Works*, ed. Hunterian Club, II, No. xxiv, p. 37), speaks scornfully of "Thou scuruie Ballat of *I wale in woe*," and in his *Good Newes*, 1622, sig. B^v, he says: "*I waile in woe*, my Knight doth *plunge in paine*." The first line is sung by the Pedant in Joshua Cooke's play, *How a Man May Choose a Good Wife from a Bad*, 1602, sig. E^v; is burlesqued in William Rowley's *Match at Midnight*, V, i, where Randall sings, "Hur wail in woe, hur plunge in pain"; and is named as a dance-tune in John Taylor the Water Poet's *An Armado, or Nauye of 103. Ships* (1627). It seems also to be imitated in the *Gorgeous Gallery*, p. 104: "They diue in dole, they plunge in payne." But more famous than these

NOTES 119

is the elaborate parody of the song by means of which Marston, Chapman, and Ben Jonson resolved the plot of their comedy, *Eastward Ho* (1605), V, v, 43 ff. In that parody, —which often appears in ballad-books (like *Wit and Drollery*, 1661, pp. 100–102) without acknowledgment to *Eastward Ho*, — Jonson probably had the chief share. It runs thus:

Quick. It is in imitation of Mannington's, he that was hanged at Cambridge, that cut off the horse's head at a blow.
Friend. So, sir!
Quick. To the tune of 'I wail in woe, I plunge in pain.'
Sir Pet. An excellent ditty it is, and worthy of a new tune.
Quick. *In Cheapside, famous for gold and plate,*
    Quicksilver, I did dwell of late;
    I had a master good and kind,
    That would have wrought me to his mind.
    He bade me still, Work upon that,
    But, alas, I wrought I knew not what!
    He was a Touchstone black, but true,
    And told me still what would ensue;
    Yet woe is me! I would not learn;
    I saw, alas, but could not discern!
Friend. Excellent, excellent well!
Gold. [*aside to* Wolf] O let him alone; he is taken already.
Quick. *I cast my coat and cap away,*
    I went in silks and satins gay;
    False metal of good manners I
    Did daily coin unlawfully.
    I scorn'd my master, being drunk;
    I kept my gelding and my punk;
    And with a knight, Sir Flash by name,
    Who now is sorry for the same —
Sir Pet. I thank you, Francis.
[*Quick.*] *I thought by sea to run away,*
    But Thames and tempest did me stay.
Touch. [*aside*] This cannot be feigned, sure. Heaven pardon my severity! The ragged colt may prove a good horse.
Gold. [*aside*] How he listens, and is transported! He has forgot me.
Quick. *Still Eastward Ho was all my word;*
    But westward I had no regard,
    Nor never thought what would come after,
    As did, alas, his youngest daughter!

> *At last the black ox trod o' my foot,*
> *And I saw then what long'd unto 't;*
> *Now cry I, ' Touchstone, touch me still,*
> *And make me current by thy skill.'*

Touch. [*aside*] And I will do it, Francis.

Wolf. [*aside to* Golding] Stay him, Master Deputy; now is the time; we shall lose the song else.

Friend. I protest it is the best that ever I heard.

Quick. How like you it, gentlemen?

All. O admirable, sir!

Quick. This stanza now following alludes to the story of Mannington, from whence I took my project for my invention.

Friend. Pray you go on, sir.

Quick.   *O Mannington, thy stories show*
> *Thou cut'st a horse-head off at a blow!*
> *But I confess, I have not the force*
> *For to cut off the head of a horse;*
> *Yet I desire this grace to win,*
> *That I may cut off the horse-head of Sin,*
> *And leave his body in the dust*
> *Of sin's highway and bogs of lust,*
> *Whereby I may take Virtue's purse,*
> *And live with her for better, for worse.*

Friend. Admirable, sir, and excellently conceited!

Quick. Alas, sir!

Touch. [*coming to* Golding *and* Wolf] Son Golding and Master Wolf, I thank you. . . . Listen, I am ravished with his repentance, and could stand here a whole prenticeship to hear him.

Friend. Forth, good sir!

Quick. This is the last, and the *Farewell.*
> *Farewell, Cheapside, farewell, sweet trade*
> *Of Goldsmiths all, that never shall fade;*
> *Farewell, dear fellow prentices all,*
> *And be you warned by my fall:*
> *Shun usurers, bawds, and dice, and drabs;*
> *Avoid them as you would French scabs.*
> *Seek not to go beyond your tether,*
> *But cut your thongs unto your leather;*
> *So shall you thrive by little and little,*
> *Scape Tyburn, Counters, and the Spital!*

In the play of *Misogonus* (A. Brandl's *Quellen des Welt-lichen Dramas*, p. 456) one of the characters sings a "songe to the tune of Labondolose Hoto," — beginning,

O mighty Jove, some pitty take
One me poore wretch for christis sake.
Greif doth me gripe, payne doth me pinch,
Willfull dispite my harte doth wrinch, —

which not only borrows Mannington's tune but also unmistakably imitates his style and diction. This imitation is important, for it makes conclusive the argument sometime ago advanced by Professor Kittredge (*Journal of Germanic Philology*, III, 339 ff.) that *Misogonus* was written, not in 1560, but about 1578. Mr. Kittredge argues that Laurence Johnson, B.A. 1573/4, M.A. 1577, of Cambridge, wrote *Misogonus;* and this indirect allusion to Mannington, who was hanged at Cambridge in 1576, serves to reinforce his argument.

The tune of *Labandalashotte* (*Labandalashot*) is used also for D. Sterrie's "A briefe sonet declaring the lamentation of Beckles," 1586 (Lilly's *Ballads*, p. 78), and for Thomas Deloney's "A New Song of King Edgar," *ca.* 1590 (*Works*, ed. F. O. Mann, p. 305). From the latter ballad, with its refrain of "call him downe a," it appears that both Mrs. Quickly (*Merry Wives*, I, iv, 44) and Ophelia (*Hamlet*, IV, v, 170) sang ballads written to this tune.

Alliteration is a noteworthy stylistic device throughout Mr. Mannington's song.

1917. *I waile in wo.* Cf. line 1641, note.
1920. *whereas. MS.* here as.
1926. *MS.* Such care my sillye soule doth keepe.
1927. *Yea. MS.* Yet.
1928. *youthful yeares. MS.* wicked wayes.
1929. *retch lesse* (cf. line 1967). Reckless. *race. MS.* care. The line means: 'I repent the reckless course of (my) careless (or care-free) nature.'
1934. *those. MS.* them.
1936. *he, thee. MS.* it, me.
1937. *nor. MS.* no.
1938. *No friendly sute. MS.* What so it be.

1943. *doom, my. MS.* dumpes, this.

1945. *And. MS.* The.

1949–58 are omitted in the MS.

1959. *friend. MS.* frendes.   *where euer. MS.* wheresoever.

1962. *Thy, is. MS.* Your, lyeth.

1966. *MS.* Bene borne and bread of meaner state.

1972. *heard. MS.* heare.

1974. *runne the race where euer.   MS.* knue the kace wheresoever.

1979 f.   Referring perhaps to the Syrtes, or quicksands on the African coast of the Mediterranean.

1985. *God. MS.* Jove.

1987. *For. MS.* In.

1990. *please. MS.* pleaseth.

1997. *doth fleet. MS.* do flitt.

No. 30, Line 2003

The tune of the *Nine muses* is unknown.   It was used for the ballad "Of the horrible and wofull destruction of Sodome and Gomorra" (Lilly's *Ballads*, p. 125) that was licensed in 1570–71 (Arber, I, 439).

The title is misleading: it really should be "A Proper Sonnet of a Damsel Who Is Unkind to Her Faithful Lover," for it is a complaint made in the first person by a man against his faithless mistress.   Possibly the obscurity of title was intentional, so that No. 30 would appear to be a new "delight."

No. 30 is a barefaced plagiarism from the Earl of Surrey's poem, "The louer describes his restlesse state" (*Tottel's Miscellany*, ed. Arber, p. 24).   Surrey's poem runs as follows, the stanza in brackets being taken from a MS. version given in F. M. Padelford's edition of Surrey (1920), p. 52:

> As oft as I behold and se
> The soueraigne bewtie that me bound:
> The nier my comfort is to me,
> Alas the fresher is my wound.

As flame doth quenche by rage of fire,
And running stremes consume by raine:
So doth the sight, that I desire,
Appease my grief and deadely paine,
[Like as the flee that seethe the flame
And thinkes to plaie her in the fier,
That fownd her woe, and sowght her game,
Whose grief did growe by her desire.]
First when I saw those cristall streames,
Whose bewtie made my mortall wound:
I little thought within her beames
So swete a venom to haue found.
But wilfull will did prick me forth,
And blind Cupide did whippe and guide:
Force made me take my griefe in worth:
My fruitles hope my harme did hide.
As cruell waues full oft be found
Against the rockes to rore and cry:
So doth my hart full oft rebound
Ageinst my brest full bitterly.
I fall, and se mine own decay,
As on that beares flame in hys brest,
Forgets in paine to put away
The thing that bredeth mine vnrest.

This plagiarism indicates an early date for No. 30, and it seems probable that the ballad was in the 1566 *Pleasant Sonnets*. In his notes Mr. Padelford shows that Surrey's poem is "a mosaic of Petrarchian lines."

2008. *neer.* Comparative, nearer (as in the third line of Surrey's poem).

No. 31, Line 2049

There is no evidence for the date of this ballad. For the tune see the introductory note to No. 15.

2078. *Read* ¶ A thousand sighs to sēd (this phrase occurs also in *Twelfth Night*, II, iv, 64; *2 Henry VI*, III, ii, 345; *Troilus and Cressida*, IV, iv, 41).

No. 32, Line 2108

The tune (cf. the introductory note on No. 27) indicates
that this ballad was probably in the 1566 *Pleasant Sonnets*.
The ballad was first reprinted in Thomas Evans's *Old Bal-
lads*, I (1810), 340.

2116. *wo ho.* The cry of a falconer in calling a falcon
back to the lure. Elizabethan dramatists used the cry con-
tinually: *e.g.*, *Hamlet*, I, v, 115 f.; Chapman's *Gentleman
Usher*, V, i, 103; Jonson, Chapman, and Marston's *Eastward
Ho*, II, i, 98; Marston's *Dutch Courtezan*, I, ii, 238, IV, v, 8,
72, 75.

2122. *bending eies.* That is, eyes looking toward him.
The falcon looks as if she were consenting, were coming to
the lure, — but away she flies.

INDEX OF FIRST LINES, TITLES
AND TUNES

*First lines and titles are printed in roman type,
and the latter are enclosed in quotation-marks.
Tunes are printed in italics.*

GLOSSARIAL INDEX

*Small roman numerals refer to pages of the Introduction;
arabic numerals in italics, to pages of the Notes; arabic
numerals in roman type, to lines of the text.*

a, prefix or preposition with participles, 288, 290, *355*
accuse, *blame, reproach*, 966
Actaeon and Diana, ballad of, 698
aglets (aiglets), *the tags of a woman's garters*, 570
Alecto, *one of the Furies*, 1661
Alexander the Great, *105.* *See* Macedon
Allen, J. W., xi
almain, 1096 n., 2051
Anaxarete, *105*
and if (an if), *provided that*, 833
Andeli, Henri d', *105*
Anders, H. R. D., v n., *88, 109*
annoy, *annoyance, trouble*, 205, 1219, 1284
apase (apace), 1029
Arber, Edward, *84, 86, 97, 104, 110, 122*; *Handful of Pleasant De-
    lights*, vi ff., xi, *73, 76*; *Stationers' Registers*, x, xii n., *81, 84f.,
    88–91, 96–100, 102f., 105ff., 110, 112f., 115–118, 122*
areed (aread), *advise*, 239
Argus eyes, 1131 n.
Aristoteles und Phillis, 105
Aristotle and Phyllis, story of, transferred to Hercules, *105f.*
as, *as if*, 1363; *that*, 1083
aspen leaf, 1393
Atropos, *one of the Fates*, 1022 (cf. 1786)
authors of the *Handful* ballads. *See* Gibson, Leonard; Hunnis,
    William; Mannington, George; P., I.; Picks, Peter; Richard-
    son, Thomas; Robinson, Clement; Tomson, I.
Axon, G. R., *92*

Babylon, 967
Bagford, John, x, *73*
baine (bane), *destruction*, 277, 631
band, *bond, promise*, 1038
Bandello, Matteo, *115*
Barclay, Alexander, *103*
be by, *be near*, 669

crocodiles' tears, 1244, 1590
Crossley, James, vii f., *76*
"Cruelty of Fortune, The," *115*
Cupid, 37, 232, 425 ff., 846, 2025, 2043
Cupid's dart, 1225; fire, 898; fort, 1259; thralls, 1280
Cupidoes (Cupido's), 437
curious and brave, *elegant and fine*, 718

"Daily Exercise of the Common Sort of Men, The," *106 f.*
dame, *mother*, 321, 1961
Damon and Pythias, 1631 n.
D'Andeli, Henri, *105*
Danea, 134 ff.
dark, *darken*, 1526
Davison, Francis, *Poetical Rhapsody*, ix
De la Peend, Thomas, *115*
decay, *destroy*, 1599; *ruin*, 1843
deemd, *judged, condemned*, 1633
Deloney, Thomas, xiv, *121*
deniance, *denial*, 902
depart, *divide, separate*, 84
Diana, 92
Diana, 814, 859; Actaeon and, a ballad, 698 n.
Diophon, 135 ff.
discriue (descrive), *describe*, 1084
disease, to drink one's own, 835 n.
dismal, *unlucky, unpropitious*, 1939
displaid (displayed), *outspread*, 825
Dodsley, Robert, *115*
doing, *actions*, 358; the wooing that's long a-, *i. e., long drawn out*, 290
doom, *sentence, judgment*, 623, 1076, 1945
doubleness, *duplicity*, 952
doubt, *hesitate, scruple*, 21 (*Printer to the Reader*), 1113
Drayton, Michael, *83*
dreed (dread), 1000
drink one's own disease, to, 835 n.
drowping (drooping), 2054
Dyboski, R., *104, 107*

Ebsworth, J. W., x, xii, *73*
Edwards, Richard, *115*. *See Paradise of Dainty Devices*
eke, *also*, 552
eke also, 71

Elderton, William, *89 f., 96, 101, 105, 112, 114, 117*
Ellis, George, vi, *90, 103*
Englands Parnassus. *See* Crawford, Charles
Ennius, *85*
ensample, *example*, 1827
Evans, Thomas, vi, *82, 85, 100, 116, 124*
euerichone, *every one*, 275

F., W., balladist, *110*
"Fain Would I Have a Virtuous Wife," *116*
"Fain Would I Have and Take no Pain," *116*
faine, *glad*, 22
Fairholt, F. W., *90*
fairings, 3 n.
falconer, ballad comparing a lover to a, 2108
Fallersleben, H. von, *103*
false, *falsify*, 1552
fancie, *love*, 324, 1272, 1321, 2084; *imagination*, 1797; *whim*, 940
fancy, *to love*, 1436
"Farewell to Alas I Love You Over Well, A," *117*
fellows, *companions, friends*, 271
fennel, 47 n.
fethered boy, *Cupid*, 1613
field, to win the, 121
filed, *polished, elaborated*, 1480
fine, in, *in conclusion*, 796
"Flattering Lover's Farewell to Nanny, The," *81*
fleet, *flit*, 1997
Fletcher, John, *87*
flinging fancies, 940 n.
flout, 356
foile, *defeat*, 177
fond, *foolish*, 424, 1267, 1280
fooles paradice, 937
for, *against, to prevent*, 489 n.
for why, 690 n.
force of, by, *because of the power of*, 867 f.
Foster, Joseph, *84*
frame, *order, plan*, 1322
free (freely), *noble (nobly), of gentle breeding*, 508, 858
friend, *lover*, 374, 1128, 1367, etc.
friendly, *in loving fashion*, 1345
friendship, *love*, 1341

froward, 671 n.
fulfil, *fill full*, 96
Fulwood, William, *110*
Furnivall, F. J., *87*, *104*

Galerent, Le Roman de, *103*
gan, *began*, 1595
Garland of Delight, The, *102*
garlands, the *Handful* as the first of the, xiv
Gascoigne, George, *104*
gases (gazes), 1692 n.
gate, *got*, 1893
gay, *fine*, *beautiful*, 574, 1400
Gayley, C. M., *87*
geare, all this, *all these things*, 601
geason, *scanty*, *lacking*, 1692
geck, to give one the, *mock or deceive*, 943
gent, *graceful*, *elegant*, 712
ghost, *spirit*, *soul*, 1193
Gibson, Leonard, ballad by, 134; facts about, *84*
gifts, *beauties (of the lips and teeth)*, 1058
gillyflowers, 81 n.
glad, *gladden*, 142
gleams, 646 n.
glee, to give one, 1830
go to! 377
"Goddess Diana, The," *91*
Golding, Arthur, *99*
"Gomorrah, The Woeful Destruction of," *122*
Gonville and Caius College. *See* Gunuil Hall
good-night, a, 1914 n.
Googe, Barnabe, *113*
Gorgeous Gallery of Gallant Inventions, A, viii, ix n., x ff.; cited, *85*,
     91, *96*, *99*, *105*; plagiarisms or imitations of the *Handful* in, xii,
     xv, *86*, *89*, *108*, *110*, *113*, *117 f*.
Gower, John, *103 f.*, *107*
gravers, *engravers*, 1707
Gray, William, ix n.
green, clothed in, 579 n.
Greene, Robert, *104*, *106*
Greensleeves, Lady, ballad on, 511 (*90*)
Grissell, Patient, *115*. *See* Phillip, John
Grosart, Alexander, *104*

MS. Percy Folio, *87*
MS. Rawlinson Poet. 108, ballads in, referred to, *98*, *116*
MS. Rawlinson Poet. 148, ballad in, quoted, *103*
marigolds, 99
Markham, Isabella, *117*
Marlborough, Duke of.   *See* Blandford
Marriage of Wit and Wisdom, The, ed. Halliwell (*q. v.*), *86*, *103*
marshall ray, *martial array*, 153
Marston, John, *119*, *124*
"Marvelous Strange Deformed Swine, A," *88*
Mendoza, Don Juan de, *115*
Midas, 1281 n.
milk, white as the, 559
mind, *perceive, notice*, 167;   *intend*, 1171
mind, to fulfil your, *carry out your wishes*, 76
Minus, 988 n.
"Miserable State of King Midas, The," *106*
misleeke, *dislike*, 1122
Misogonus.   *See* Johnson, Laurence
miss, *lack, privation*, 790
mo, *more*, 806
momish mates, *foolish fellows*, 1281
moralized ballads, *90*, *98*, *100 f.*, *116*
more dearer, 1803
Mowntayne, Thomas, *104*
moyling, *toiling*, 1812
much ado, 1890
Munday, Anthony, *100*
muses, the nine, 655, 963, 1045, 1736, 2003 n.
My Lord Marquis's Galliard, 112

Narcissus, ballad on, 786 (*97*)
Nashe, Thomas, *105*
naturally, *by nature*, 875
ne, *a negative*, 449, 477, 479, 1063, 1190, 2079
neer, *nearer*, 2008 n.
Nestor, 1839
"New Ballad of One Misliking His Liberty, A," *88*
"New Sonnet Showing How Diana Transformed Actaeon, A," *92*
Newton, Thomas, *82*
nice, *coquettish, disdainful*, 632;   to make a matter, *display reluctance*,
    936
Nichols, J. G., *104*

Peele, Stephen, *100*
Peend, Thomas de la, *115*
peeuish, *senseless, foolish*, 1279
peise, *weigh, consider*, 1872
Penelope, 1857
peniriall, *pennyroyal*, 107
Pepys, Samuel, ballad-collection of, cited, *81*
Percy, Bishop Thomas, folio MS. of, *87*
Perry Library, vi
Phillip, John, *100, 102, 115*
"Philosophers' Learnings Are Full of Good Warnings," *112*
Phoebus' light, *the sun*, 1083
Phyllis and Aristotle, *105 f.*
Picks, Peter, ballads by, ?287 *(86)*, 354 n.
pies, *magpies*, 2130
Pikering, John, *98*
pillow, make much of one's, *take counsel of one's pillow, 'sleep upon'*
    a question, 352
pincase, 553
Piramus. *See* Pyramus
Pitt(s), John, ballad possibly by, *88*
"Pleasant Posy or Sweet Nosegay, A," *81*
Poetical Rhapsody, A. See Davison, Francis
poisoned, *malignant*, 1654
Porter, Henry, *Two Angry Women*, *87*
praie (prey), 1003
preeue, *prove*, 1441
Preston, Thomas, *106*
Priam, 1620 n.; his son, *Paris*, 1267
price (prize), *the golden apple*, 1268
prick on a clout, *sew*, 380
prime, *the first hour of the day, sunrise*, 987; the golden, *youth*, 201
printers: Allde, Edward, *107*; Allde, John, *99*; Cherlewood, John,
    81; Colwell, Thomas, *91*; Griffith, William, *99* f., *103, 107, 117*;
    Hudson, Richard, *115*; Jones, Richard, ix f., xiii, *88, 90, 97, 102,
    118*; King, John, *81*; Lacy, Alexander, *91, 98*; Pekering, Wil-
    liam, *91, 107*; Tottel, Richard, *105*; Wright, Edward, *81*;
    Wright, John, *92*
Proctor, Thomas. *See Gorgeous Gallery*
proverbs: beat the bush, miss the birds, 1381 n.; cat winks but is
    not blind, 1134 n.; chip falls in one's eye when one looks too high,
    1299 n.; fast bind, fast find, 1241 n.; first try, then trust, 1266
    n.; fish fair and catch a frog, 1127 n.; had I wist, 1240 n.; hot

love is soon cold, 307 n.; leech, the, comes too late when the patient is dead, *103;* lingering love brings misliking, *103;* look ere you leap, 1255 n.; of grass comes hay, 1289 n.; rule the roast, 1263 n.; snake, the, lies in the grass, 235 n.; soon ripe, soon rotten, 1291 n.; spare to speak, fail to speed, 483 n.; tide tarrieth no man, 332 n.; time trieth all things, 65 n.; try before you trust, 1266 n.; when the steed is stolen, it 's too late to shut the stable door, 1237 n.; wooing that 's not long a-doing is blessed, 290 n.; words are wind, 1373 n.

Proverbes del Vilain, Les, 104

pumps, *light shoes,* 559

Puttenham, George, *84*

Pyramus and Thisbe, 99

Pyramus and Thisbe, ballad on, 957 n.; mentioned, *99,* 1276, 1565, 1576, 1620 n. (*i. e., Priam*)

Pythias, 1631 n.

Quarter braules, 698 n.

Qui passa, 112

quite, *requite, repay,* 1342

R., C. (Robinson, Clement?), xiv

race, *course, career,* 171 n., 202, 284, 1929, 1951

Rare and greatest gift, The, 85

ray, *array,* 153

rechlesse (retchless), *heedless, careless,* 1929, 1967

regard, *to be inclined to or desirous of,* 19 (*Printer to the Reader*); *care for (love)* one, 882

Reliquiae Antiquae, ed. Wright and Halliwell (*q. v.*), *104*

remorce (remorse), *compassion,* 680

remove, *change,* 652, 800

rent, *rend,* 1589 n.

require, *ask for, request,* 26, 776, 928, 1114, 1603

retchless. *See* rechlesse

retire, *retirement, withdrawal,* 899

revengement, 1941

Richardson ('Richeson'), Thomas, ballads by, *85,* 285

Ritson, Joseph, v, x, *84, 118*

Robinson, Clement, compiler of the *Handful,* probable author of most of its unsigned ballads, v, x, xiv

Rogero, 92

Rollins, H. E., *84, 92, 96, 98, 100 f., 116*

Romeus (Romeo), 1275 n.

rosemary, 31 n.

sirens, 1243
Siria (Syria), 175
sisters three, *the Fates (Clotho, Lachesis, Atropos)*, 1786 (cf. 1022)
sith, *since*, 638, 1743, 2052
sithence, *since*, 676
slacking, *slackening, becoming less*, 345
slenderly (adjective), 895
smack, *kiss noisily*, 243
smart, *pain, anguish*, 231, 416, 640, etc.
"Smelling Nosegay, A," *81*
smirke, *smirking, smiling*, 644
snuffe, *show disdain*, 1154
"Sodom and Gomorrah, The Woeful Destruction of," *122*
sonet (sonnet), *a song, short poem, or ballad (never the rigid fourteen-line poem)*, passim
sort, *class (of people)*, 129, 1297; *manner*, 713 f.
space, *while, time*, 1879
sped, to be, *succeed in obtaining (a lover) for oneself*, 1103, 1108
speed, *prosper, succeed*, 1733
Spenser, Edmund, *83, 104*
spill, *destroy, ruin*, 1446, 1940
sprung, *produced*, 13
squats and flats, *used of a hart which squats or lies flat on the ground when pursued*, 922
stay, *restrain*, 673, 1608
Sterrie, D., *121*
still, 41 n.
stoong (stung), 1661
Stopes, Mrs. C. C., *82*
stroke, strook (struck), 846, 1881
Stucley, The Play of, 87
"Subtle Simon," *102*
Surrey, Earl of (Howard, Henry), *110, 122*
Susanna and the Elders, 1653 n.
suspect, *suspicion*, 1862
suspected, *suspicious*, 1668
sway, to bear no, *exert no influence*, 1260
Syria, 175
Syrtes, the, 1979 n.

tantara (taratantara), 134 n.
Taylor, John, the Water Poet, *118*
Teucer, King, *105*

than, *then*, 1558, 1715
that, *what*, 318, 331, 671, 1160, 1270, 1282, 1689
the (thee), 1886
then, *than*, 1731, 1840
tho, *then*, 1744
threed (thread) of Atropos, 1022; of all the Fates, 1787
throughly, *thoroughly*, 1424
thyme. *See* time
tide, *time*, 332
time (thyme), 65 n.
to, *as*, 1481; *for*, 91, 530, 1627
toad, a venomous, 1310 n.
tofore, *formerly*, 1670
Tomson, I., ballads by, 839 n., 910, 1049
too too, *exceedingly*, 1927
toss the cup, *to drink (beer, wine)*, 1283
Tottel's Miscellany, ix, xi, xv; ballads in, imitated in the *Handful*,
    110, 114, 116, 122; cited, *86, 97, 104*
toyes (toys), *trifles, matters of no importance*, 1599, 1863
trace, *track or trail (of a hart)*, 918
trade, *the tread of (Fortune's) wheel*, 1976
train, *followers*, 1971; *tail*, 2140
"Translated Tantura of Transitories, A," *84*
trim shifter, *neat or clever trickster*, 401
trips, *snares (of Cupid)*, 1248; and skips, *describing the running of a
    hart when pursued*, 921
Troylus (Troilus), *98, 116*, 871, 1274, 1620
trudging, 387
"True Report in the Praise of My Mistress, A," *98*
Turbervile, George, *104*
turtle, *the dove*, 625, 1451
Tusser, Thomas, *104*
twist, *thread*, 293 n.

vade, *fade, pass away*, 1025
vailes, *profit, gain*, 1288
venerie (venery), *hunting*, 846
Venn, John, *85*
Venus, 760 n., 799, 833, 860, 869, 928, 1077, 1251, 1268, 1736; the
    power of, ballad on, 758 ff.
viewd, to, 995 n.
violet, 55
Virgil, *86, 106, 113*

Virginia, 81
virginity, ballad in praise of, 1170
Ulysses, 1245; his wife, *Penelope*, 1857
unclothe, *reveal*, 984
"Unfortunate End of Iphis, The," *105*
unneth, *with difficulty*, 1573
"Unthrifts, A New Ballad against," *110*
use, *conduct oneself*, 104 n.; *practise*, 816 n.; *be accustomed*, 1303,
    1311

waged, *pledged*, 527
Wager, Lewis, *109*
waiest (weighest), *dost value*, 432
Ward, H. L. D., *106*
watered, *tearful*, 1473
wax, *grow*, 307
way (weigh), *consider*, 1597, 1755
weare (were), 726
Webbe, William, *100*
weid (weighed), 1396
well bent, *of good disposition or intention*, 1317
went still about her, *kept seeking after (wooing) her*, 289
Wesselski, A., *106*
whan (when), 955
where, *whereas*, 413, 1157
Where is the life of late, 102
whereas, *where*, 1508, 1789, 1920
Whetstone, George, *111*
white, hit the, *hit the center or mark at which an arrow is aimed, i. e.,
    to succeed*, 1380
white as the milk, 559
White Knights Library, v f.
wiles (wills), *impels*, 1816
wish and have, to, 6 n. (*Printer to the Reader*)
Wit and Drollery, 119
Wither, George, xiii
withouten (without), 16
wo ho, 2116 n., 2126 ff.
woe worth, *woe be to*, 1595
worms, *young people*, 1217
"Worthy Mirror, A," *118*
wrack (wreck), *ruin*, 1399, 1596
wreathed, *encircling*, 1800

CATALOGUE OF DOVER BOOKS

Literature, History of Literature

ARISTOTLE'S THEORY OF POETRY AND THE FINE ARTS, edited by S. H. Butcher. The celebrated Butcher translation of this great classic faced, page by page, with the complete Greek text. A 300 page introduction discussing Aristotle's ideas and their influence in the history of thought and literature, and covering art and nature, imitation as an aesthetic form, poetic truth, art and morality, tragedy, comedy, and similar topics. Modern Aristotelian criticism discussed by John Gassner. lxxvi + 421pp. 5⅜ x 8. T42 Paperbound **$2.00**

INTRODUCTIONS TO ENGLISH LITERATURE, edited by B. Dobrée. Goes far beyond ordinary histories, ranging from the 7th century up to 1914 (to the 1940's in some cases.) The first half of each volume is a specific detailed study of historical and economic background of the period and a general survey of poetry and prose, including trends of thought, influences, etc. The second and larger half is devoted to a detailed study of more than 5000 poets, novelists, dramatists; also economists, historians, biographers, religious writers, philosophers, travellers, and scientists of literary stature, with dates, lists of major works and their dates, keypoint critical bibliography, and evaluating comments. The most compendious bibliographic and literary aid within its price range.

Vol. I. THE BEGINNINGS OF ENGLISH LITERATURE TO SKELTON, (1509), W. L. Renwick, H. Orton. 450pp. 5⅛ x 7⅞. T75 Clothbound **$4.50**

Vol. II. THE ENGLISH RENAISSANCE, 1510-1688, V. de Sola Pinto. 381pp. 5⅛ x 7⅞. T76 Clothbound **$4.50**

Vol. III. AUGUSTANS AND ROMANTICS, 1689-1830, H. Dyson, J. Butt. 320pp. 5⅛ x 7⅞. T77 Clothbound **$4.50**

Vol. IV. THE VICTORIANS AND AFTER, 1830-1940's, E. Batho, B. Dobrée. 360pp. 5⅛ x 7⅞. T78 Clothbound **$4.50**

EPIC AND ROMANCE, W. P. Ker. Written by one of the foremost authorities on medieval literature, this is the standard survey of medieval epic and romance. It covers Teutonic epics, Icelandic sagas, Beowulf, French chansons de geste, the Roman de Troie, and many other important works of literature. It is an excellent account for a body of literature whose beauty and value has only recently come to be recognized. Index. xxiv + 398pp. 5⅜ x 8. T355 Paperbound **$2.00**

THE POPULAR BALLAD, F. B. Gummere. Most useful factual introduction; fund of descriptive material; quotes, cites over 260 ballads. Examines, from folkloristic view, structure; choral, ritual elements; meter, diction, fusion; effects of tradition, editors; almost every other aspect of border, riddle, kinship, sea, ribald, supernatural, etc., ballads. Bibliography. 2 indexes. 374pp. 5⅜ x 8. T548 Paperbound **$1.85**

MASTERS OF THE DRAMA, John Gassner. The most comprehensive history of the drama in print, covering drama in every important tradition from the Greeks to the Near East, China, Japan, Medieval Europe, England, Russia, Italy, Spain, Germany, and dozens of other drama producing nations. This unsurpassed reading and reference work encompasses more than 800 dramatists and over 2000 plays, with biographical material, plot summaries, theatre history, etc. "Has no competitors in its field," THEATRE ARTS. "Best of its kind in English," NEW REPUBLIC. Exhaustive 35 page bibliography. 77 photographs and drawings. Deluxe edition with reinforced cloth binding, headbands, stained top. xxii + 890pp. 5⅜ x 8. T100 Clothbound **$6.95**

THE DEVELOPMENT OF DRAMATIC ART, D. C. Stuart. The basic work on the growth of Western drama from primitive beginnings to Eugene O'Neill, covering over 2500 years. Not a mere listing or survey, but a thorough analysis of changes, origins of style, and influences in each period; dramatic conventions, social pressures, choice of material, plot devices, stock situations, etc.; secular and religious works of all nations and epochs. "Generous and thoroughly documented researches," Outlook. "Solid studies of influences and playwrights and periods," London Times. Index. Bibliography. xi + 679pp. 5⅜ x 8. T693 Paperbound **$2.75**

A SOURCE BOOK IN THEATRICAL HISTORY (SOURCES OF THEATRICAL HISTORY), A. M. Nagler. Over 2000 years of actors, directors, designers, critics, and spectators speak for themselves in this potpourri of writings selected from the great and formative periods of western drama. On-the-spot descriptions of masks, costumes, makeup, rehearsals, special effects, acting methods, backstage squabbles, theatres, etc. Contemporary glimpses of Molière rehearsing his company, an exhortation to a Roman audience to buy refreshments and keep quiet, Goethe's rules for actors, Belasco telling of $6500 he spent building a river, Restoration actors being told to avoid "lewd, obscene, or indecent postures," and much more. Each selection has an introduction by Prof. Nagler. This extraordinary, lively collection is ideal as a source of otherwise difficult to obtain material, as well as a fine book for browsing. Over 80 illustrations. 10 diagrams. xxiii + 611pp. 5⅜ x 8. T515 Paperbound **$3.00**

CATALOGUE OF DOVER BOOKS

WORLD DRAMA, B. H. Clark. The dramatic creativity of a score of ages and eras — all in two handy compact volumes. Over ⅓ of this material is unavailable in any other current edition! 46 plays from Ancient Greece, Rome, Medieval Europe, France, Germany, Italy, England, Russia, Scandinavia, India, China, Japan, etc. — including classic authors like Aeschylus, Sophocles, Euripides, Aristophanes, Plautus, Marlowe, Jonson, Farquhar, Goldsmith, Cervantes, Molière, Dumas, Goethe, Schiller, Ibsen, and many others. This creative collection avoids hackneyed material and includes only completely first-rate works which are relatively little known or difficult to obtain. "The most comprehensive collection of important plays from all literature available in English," SAT. REV. OF LITERATURE. Introduction. Reading lists. 2 volumes. 1364pp. 5⅜ x 8.

Vol. 1, T57 Paperbound **$2.25**
Vol. 2, T59 Paperbound **$2.50**

MASTERPIECES OF THE RUSSIAN DRAMA, edited with introduction by G. R. Noyes. This only comprehensive anthology of Russian drama ever published in English offers complete texts, in 1st-rate modern translations, of 12 plays covering 200 years. Vol. 1: "The Young Hopeful," Fonvisin; "Wit Works Woe," Griboyedov; "The Inspector General," Gogol; "A Month in the Country," Turgenev; "The Poor Bride," Ostrovsky; "A Bitter Fate," Pisemsky. Vol. 2: "The Death of Ivan the Terrible," Alexey Tolstoy "The Power of Darkness," Lev Tolstoy; "The Lower Depths," Gorky; "The Cherry Orchard," Chekhov; "Professor Storitsyn," Andreyev; "Mystery Bouffe," Mayakovsky. Bibliography. Total of 902pp. 5⅜ x 8.

Vol. 1 T647 Paperbound **$2.00**
Vol. 2 T648 Paperbound **$2.00**

EUGENE O'NEILL: THE MAN AND HIS PLAYS, B. H. Clark. Introduction to O'Neill's life and work. Clark analyzes each play from the early THE WEB to the recently produced MOON FOR THE MISBEGOTTEN and THE ICEMAN COMETH revealing the environmental and dramatic influences necessary for a complete understanding of these important works. Bibliography. Appendices. Index. ix + 182pp. 5⅜ x 8.
T379 Paperbound **$1.35**

THE HEART OF THOREAU'S JOURNALS, edited by O. Shepard. The best general selection from Thoreau's voluminous (and rare) journals. This intimate record of thoughts and observations reveals the full Thoreau and his intellectual development more accurately than any of his published works: self-conflict between the scientific observer and the poet, reflections on transcendental philosophy, involvement in the tragedies of neighbors and national causes, etc. New preface, notes, introductions. xii + 228pp. 5⅜ x 8.
T741 Paperbound **$1.50**

H. D. THOREAU: A WRITER'S JOURNAL, edited by L. Stapleton. A unique new selection from the Journals concentrating on Thoreau's growth as a conscious literary artist, the ideals and purposes of his art. Most of the material has never before appeared outside of the complete 14-volume edition. Contains vital insights on Thoreau's projected book on Concord, thoughts on the nature of men and government, indignation with slavery, sources of inspiration, goals in life. Index. xxxiii + 234pp. 5⅜ x 8.
T678 Paperbound **$1.65**

THE HEART OF EMERSON'S JOURNALS, edited by Bliss Perry. Best of these revealing Journals, originally 10 volumes, presented in a one volume edition. Talks with Channing, Hawthorne, Thoreau, and Bronson Alcott; impressions of Webster, Everett, John Brown, and Lincoln; records of moments of sudden understanding, vision, and solitary ecstasy. "The essays do not reveal the power of Emerson's mind . . . as do these hasty and informal writings," N.Y. Times. Preface by Bliss Perry. Index. xiii + 357pp. 5⅜ x 8.   T477 Paperbound **$1.85**

FOUNDERS OF THE MIDDLE AGES, E. K. Rand. This is the best non-technical discussion of the transformation of Latin pagan culture into medieval civilization. Covering such figures as Tertullian, Gregory, Jerome, Boethius, Augustine, the Neoplatonists, and many other literary men, educators, classicists, and humanists, this book is a storehouse of information presented clearly and simply for the intelligent non-specialist. "Thoughtful, beautifully written," AMERICAN HISTORICAL REVIEW. "Extraordinarily accurate," Richard McKeon, THE NATION. ix + 365pp. 5⅜ x 8.
T369 Paperbound **$2.00**

PLAY-MAKING: A MANUAL OF CRAFTSMANSHIP, William Archer. With an extensive, new introduction by John Gassner, Yale Univ. The permanently essential requirements of solid play construction are set down in clear, practical language: theme, exposition, foreshadowing, tension, obligatory scene, peripety, dialogue, character, psychology, other topics. This book has been one of the most influential elements in the modern theatre, and almost everything said on the subject since is contained explicitly or implicitly within its covers. Bibliography. Index. xlii + 277pp. 5⅜ x 8.
T651 Paperbound **$1.75**

HAMBURG DRAMATURGY, G. E. Lessing. One of the most brilliant of German playwrights of the eighteenth-century age of criticism analyzes the complex of theory and tradition that constitutes the world of theater. These 104 essays on aesthetic theory helped demolish the regime of French classicism, opening the door to psychological and social realism, romanticism. Subjects include the original functions of tragedy; drama as the rational world; the meaning of pity and fear, pity and fear as means for purgation and other Aristotelian concepts; genius and creative force; interdependence of poet's language and actor's interpretation; truth and authenticity; etc. A basic and enlightening study for anyone interested in aesthetics and ideas, from the philosopher to the theatergoer. Introduction by Prof. Victor Lange. xxii + 265pp. 4½ x 6⅜.
T32 Paperbound **$1.45**

Language Books and Records

GERMAN: HOW TO SPEAK AND WRITE IT. AN INFORMAL CONVERSATIONAL METHOD FOR SELF STUDY, Joseph Rosenberg. Eminently useful for self study because of concentration on elementary stages of learning. Also provides teachers with remarkable variety of aids: 28 full- and double-page sketches with pertinent items numbered and identified in German and English; German proverbs, jokes; grammar, idiom studies; extensive practice exercises. The most interesting introduction to German available, full of amusing illustrations, photographs of cities and landmarks in German-speaking cities, cultural information subtly woven into conversational material. Includes summary of grammar, guide to letter writing, study guide to German literature by Dr. Richard Friedenthal. Index. 400 illustrations. 384pp. 5⅜ x 8½.
T271 Paperbound **$2.00**

FRENCH: HOW TO SPEAK AND WRITE IT. AN INFORMAL CONVERSATIONAL METHOD FOR SELF STUDY, Joseph Lemaitre. Even the absolute beginner can acquire a solid foundation for further study from this delightful elementary course. Photographs, sketches and drawings, sparkling colloquial conversations on a wide variety of topics (including French culture and custom), French sayings and quips, are some of aids used to demonstrate rather than merely describe the language. Thorough yet surprisingly entertaining approach, excellent for teaching and for self study. Comprehensive analysis of pronunciation, practice exercises and appendices of verb tables, additional vocabulary, other useful material. Index. Appendix. 400 illustrations. 416pp. 5⅜ x 8½.
T268 Paperbound **$2.00**

DICTIONARY OF SPOKEN SPANISH, Spanish-English, English-Spanish. Compiled from spoken Spanish, emphasizing idiom and colloquial usage in both Castilian and Latin-American. More than 16,000 entries containing over 25,000 idioms—the largest list of idiomatic constructions ever published. Complete sentences given, indexed under single words—language in immediately useable form, for travellers, businessmen, students, etc. 25 page introduction provides rapid survey of sounds, grammar, syntax, with full consideration of irregular verbs. Especially apt in modern treatment of phrases and structure. 17 page glossary gives translations of geographical names, money values, numbers, national holidays, important street signs, useful expressions of high frequency, plus unique 7 page glossary of Spanish and Spanish-American foods and dishes. Originally published as War Department Technical Manual TM 30-900. iv + 513pp. 5⅜ x 8.
T495 Paperbound **$1.75**

SPEAK MY LANGUAGE: SPANISH FOR YOUNG BEGINNERS, M. Ahlman, Z. Gilbert. Records provide one of the best, and most entertaining, methods of introducing a foreign language to children. Within the framework of a train trip from Portugal to Spain, an English-speaking child is introduced to Spanish by a native companion. (Adapted from a successful radio program of the N. Y. State Educational Department.) Though a continuous story, there are a dozen specific categories of expressions, including greetings, numbers, time, weather, food, clothes, family members, etc. Drill is combined with poetry and contextual use. Authentic background music is heard. An accompanying book enables a reader to follow the records, and includes a vocabulary of over 350 recorded expressions. Two 10" 33⅓ records, total of 40 minutes. Book. 40 illustrations. 69pp. 5¼ x 10½.
T890 The set **$4.95**

AN ENGLISH-FRENCH-GERMAN-SPANISH WORD FREQUENCY DICTIONARY, H. S. Eaton. An indispensable language study aid, this is a semantic frequency list of the 6000 most frequently used words in 4 languages—24,000 words in all. The lists, based on concepts rather than words alone, and containing all modern, exact, and idiomatic vocabulary, are arranged side by side to form a unique 4-language dictionary. A simple key indicates the importance of the individual words within each language. Over 200 pages of separate indexes for each language enable you to locate individual words at a glance. Will help language teachers and students, authors of textbooks, grammars, and language tests to compare concepts in the various languages and to concentrate on basic vocabulary, avoiding uncommon and obsolete words. 2 Appendixes. xxi + 441pp. 6½ x 9¼.
T738 Paperbound **$2.45**

NEW RUSSIAN-ENGLISH AND ENGLISH-RUSSIAN DICTIONARY, M. A. O'Brien. Over 70,000 entries in the new orthography! Many idiomatic uses and colloquialisms which form the basis of actual speech. Irregular verbs, perfective and imperfective aspects, regular and irregular sound changes, and other features. One of the few dictionaries where accent changes within the conjugation of verbs and the declension of nouns are fully indicated. "One of the best," Prof. E. J. Simmons, Cornell. First names, geographical terms, bibliography, etc. 738pp. 4½ x 6¼.
T208 Paperbound **$2.00**

96 MOST USEFUL PHRASES FOR TOURISTS AND STUDENTS in English, French, Spanish, German, Italian. A handy folder you'll want to carry with you. How to say "Excuse me," "How much is it?", "Write it down, please," etc., in four foreign languages. Copies limited, no more than 1 to a customer.
FREE

CATALOGUE OF DOVER BOOKS

Say It language phrase books

These handy phrase books (128 to 196 pages each) make grammatical drills unnecessary for an elementary knowledge of a spoken foreign language. Covering most matters of travel and everyday life each volume contains:

Over 1000 phrases and sentences in immediately useful forms — foreign language plus English.

Modern usage designed for Americans. Specific phrases like, "Give me small change," and "Please call a taxi."

Simplified phonetic transcription you will be able to read at sight.

The only completely indexed phrase books on the market.

Covers scores of important situations: — Greetings, restaurants, sightseeing, useful expressions, etc.

These books are prepared by native linguists who are professors at Columbia, N.Y.U., Fordham and other great universities. Use them independently or with any other book or record course. They provide a supplementary living element that most other courses lack. Individual volumes in:

Russian 75¢	Italian 75¢	Spanish 75¢	German 75¢
Hebrew 75¢	Danish 75¢	Japanese 75¢	Swedish 75¢
Dutch 75¢	Esperanto 75¢	Modern Greek 75¢	Portuguese 75¢
Norwegian 75¢	Polish 75¢	French 75¢	Yiddish 75¢
Turkish 75¢		English for German-speaking people 75¢	
English for Italian-speaking people 75¢		English for Spanish-speaking people 75¢	

Large clear type. 128-196 pages each. 3½ x 5¼. Sturdy paper binding.

Listen and Learn language records

LISTEN & LEARN is the only language record course designed especially to meet your travel and everyday needs. It is available in separate sets for FRENCH, SPANISH, GERMAN, JAPANESE, RUSSIAN, MODERN GREEK, PORTUGUESE, ITALIAN and HEBREW, and each set contains three 33⅓ rpm long-playing records—1½ hours of recorded speech by eminent native speakers who are professors at Columbia, New York University, Queens College.

Check the following special features found only in LISTEN & LEARN:

- **Dual-language recording.** 812 selected phrases and sentences, over 3200 words, spoken first in English, then in their foreign language equivalents. A suitable pause follows each foreign phrase, allowing you time to repeat the expression. You learn by unconscious assimilation.

- **128 to 206-page manual** contains everything on the records, plus a simple phonetic pronunciation guide.

- **Indexed for convenience. The only set on the market** that is completely indexed. No more puzzling over where to find the phrase you need. Just look in the rear of the manual.

- **Practical.** No time wasted on material you can find in any grammar. LISTEN & LEARN covers central core material with phrase approach. Ideal for the person with limited learning time.

- **Living, modern expressions,** not found in other courses. Hygienic products, modern equipment, shopping—expressions used every day, like "nylon" and "air-conditioned."

- **Limited objective.** Everything you learn, no matter where you stop, is immediately useful. You have to finish other courses, wade through grammar and vocabulary drill, before they help you.

- **High-fidelity recording.** LISTEN & LEARN records equal in clarity and surface-silence any record on the market costing up to $6.

"Excellent . . . the spoken records . . . impress me as being among the very best on the market," **Prof. Mario Pei,** Dept. of Romance Languages, Columbia University. "Inexpensive and well-done . . . it would make an ideal present," CHICAGO SUNDAY TRIBUNE. "More genuinely helpful than anything of its kind which I have previously encountered," **Sidney Clark,** well-known author of "ALL THE BEST" travel books.

UNCONDITIONAL GUARANTEE. Try LISTEN & LEARN, then return it within 10 days for full refund if you are not satisfied.

Each set contains three twelve-inch 33⅓ records, manual, and album.

SPANISH	the set $5.95	GERMAN	the set $5.95
FRENCH	the set $5.95	ITALIAN	the set $5.95
RUSSIAN	the set $5.95	JAPANESE	the set $5.95
PORTUGUESE	the set $5.95	MODERN GREEK	the set $5.95
MODERN HEBREW	the set $5.95		

CATALOGUE OF DOVER BOOKS

Trubner Colloquial Manuals

These unusual books are members of the famous Trubner series of colloquial manuals. They have been written to provide adults with a sound colloquial knowledge of a foreign language, and are suited for either class use or self-study. Each book is a complete course in itself, with progressive, easy to follow lessons. Phonetics, grammar, and syntax are covered, while hundreds of phrases and idioms, reading texts, exercises, and vocabulary are included. These books are unusual in being neither skimpy nor overdetailed in grammatical matters, and in presenting up-to-date, colloquial, and practical phrase material. Bilingual presentation is stressed, to make thorough self-study easier for the reader.

COLLOQUIAL HINDUSTANI, A. H. Harley, formerly Nizam's Reader in Urdu, U. of London. 30 pages on phonetics and scripts (devanagari & Arabic-Persian) are followed by 29 lessons, including material on English and Arabic-Persian influences. Key to all exercises. Vocabulary. 5 x 7½. 147pp. Clothbound $1.75

COLLOQUIAL PERSIAN, L. P. Elwell-Sutton. Best introduction to modern Persian, with 90 page grammatical section followed by conversations, 35-page vocabulary. 139pp. Clothbound $1.75

COLLOQUIAL ARABIC, DeLacy O'Leary. Foremost Islamic scholar covers language of Egypt, Syria, Palestine, & Northern Arabia. Extremely clear coverage of complex Arabic verbs & noun plurals; also cultural aspects of language. Vocabulary. xviii + 192pp. 5 x 7½. Clothbound $2.50

COLLOQUIAL GERMAN, P. F. Doring. Intensive thorough coverage of grammar in easily-followed form. Excellent for brush-up, with hundreds of colloquial phrases. 34 pages of bilingual texts. 224pp. 5 x 7½. Clothbound $1.75

COLLOQUIAL SPANISH, W. R. Patterson. Castilian grammar and colloquial language, loaded with bilingual phrases and colloquialisms. Excellent for review or self-study. 164pp. 5 x 7½. Clothbound $1.75

COLLOQUIAL FRENCH, W. R. Patterson. 16th revision of this extremely popular manual. Grammar explained with model clarity, and hundreds of useful expressions and phrases; exercises, reading texts, etc. Appendixes of new and useful words and phrases. 223pp. 5 x 7½. Clothbound $1.75

COLLOQUIAL CZECH, J. Schwarz, former headmaster of Lingua Institute, Prague. Full easily followed coverage of grammar, hundreds of immediately useable phrases, texts. Perhaps the best Czech grammar in print. "An absolutely successful textbook," JOURNAL OF CZECHO-SLOVAK FORCES IN GREAT BRITAIN. 252pp. 5 x 7½. Clothbound $3.00

COLLOQUIAL RUMANIAN, G. Nandris, Professor of University of London. Extremely thorough coverage of phonetics, grammar, syntax; also included 70-page reader, and 70-page vocabulary. Probably the best grammar for this increasingly important language. 340pp. 5 x 7½. Clothbound $2.50

COLLOQUIAL ITALIAN, A. L. Hayward. Excellent self-study course in grammar, vocabulary, idioms, and reading. Easy progressive lessons will give a good working knowledge of Italian in the shortest possible time. 5 x 7½. Clothbound $1.75

COLLOQUIAL TURKISH, Yusuf Mardin. Very clear, thorough introduction to leading cultural and economic language of Near East. Begins with pronunciation and statement of vowel harmony, then 36 lessons present grammar, graded vocabulary, useful phrases, dialogues, reading, exercises. Key to exercises at rear. Turkish-English vocabulary. All in Roman alphabet. x + 288pp. 4¾ x 7¼. Clothbound $4.00

DUTCH-ENGLISH AND ENGLISH-DUTCH DICTIONARY, F. G. Renier. For travel, literary, scientific or business Dutch, you will find this the most convenient, practical and comprehensive dictionary on the market. More than 60,000 entries, shades of meaning, colloquialisms, idioms, compounds and technical terms. Dutch and English strong and irregular verbs. This is the only dictionary in its size and price range that indicates the gender of nouns. New orthography. xvii + 571pp. 5½ x 6¼. T224 Clothbound $2.75

LEARN DUTCH, F. G. Renier. This book is the most satisfactory and most easily used grammar of modern Dutch. The student is gradually led from simple lessons in pronunciation, through translation from and into Dutch, and finally to a mastery of spoken and written Dutch. Grammatical principles are clearly explained while a useful, practical vocabulary is introduced in easy exercises and readings. It is used and recommended by the Fulbright Committee in the Netherlands. Phonetic appendices. Over 1200 exercises; Dutch-English, English-Dutch vocabularies. 181pp. 4¼ x 7¼. T441 Clothbound $2.25

Philosophy, Religion

GUIDE TO PHILOSOPHY, C. E. M. Joad. A modern classic which examines many crucial problems which man has pondered through the ages: Does free will exist? Is there plan in the universe? How do we know and validate our knowledge? Such opposed solutions as subjective idealism and realism, chance and teleology, vitalism and logical positivism, are evaluated and the contributions of the great philosophers from the Greeks to moderns like Russell, Whitehead, and others, are considered in the context of each problem. "The finest introduction," BOSTON TRANSCRIPT. Index. Classified bibliography. 592pp. 5⅜ x 8.
T297 Paperbound **$2.00**

HISTORY OF ANCIENT PHILOSOPHY, W. Windelband. One of the clearest, most accurate comprehensive surveys of Greek and Roman philosophy. Discusses ancient philosophy in general, intellectual life in Greece in the 7th and 6th centuries B.C., Thales, Anaximander, Anaximenes, Heraclitus, the Eleatics, Empedocles, Anaxagoras, Leucippus, the Pythagoreans, the Sophists, Socrates, Democritus (20 pages), Plato (50 pages), Aristotle (70 pages), the Peripatetics, Stoics, Epicureans, Sceptics, Neo-platonists, Christian Apologists, etc. 2nd German edition translated by H. E. Cushman. xv + 393pp. 5⅜ x 8.
T357 Paperbound **$1.85**

ILLUSTRATIONS OF THE HISTORY OF MEDIEVAL THOUGHT AND LEARNING, R. L. Poole. Basic analysis of the thought and lives of the leading philosophers and ecclesiastics from the 8th to the 14th century—Abailard, Ockham, Wycliffe, Marsiglio of Padua, and many other great thinkers who carried the torch of Western culture and learning through the "Dark Ages": political, religious, and metaphysical views. Long a standard work for scholars and one of the best introductions to medieval thought for beginners. Index. 10 Appendices. xiii + 327pp. 5⅜ x 8.
T674 Paperbound **$1.85**

PHILOSOPHY AND CIVILIZATION IN THE MIDDLE AGES, M. de Wulf. This semi-popular survey covers aspects of medieval intellectual life such as religion, philosophy, science, the arts, etc. It also covers feudalism vs. Catholicism, rise of the universities, mendicant orders, monastic centers, and similar topics. Unabridged. Bibliography. Index. viii + 320pp. 5⅜ x 8.
T284 Paperbound **$1.85**

AN INTRODUCTION TO SCHOLASTIC PHILOSOPHY, Prof. M. de Wulf. Formerly entitled SCHOLASTICISM OLD AND NEW, this volume examines the central scholastic tradition from St. Anselm, Albertus Magnus, Thomas Aquinas, up to Suarez in the 17th century. The relation of scholasticism to ancient and medieval philosophy and science in general is clear and easily followed. The second part of the book considers the modern revival of scholasticism, the Louvain position, relations with Kantianism and Positivism. Unabridged. xvi + 271pp. 5⅜ x 8.
T296 Clothbound **$3.50**
T283 Paperbound **$1.75**

A HISTORY OF MODERN PHILOSOPHY, H. Höffding. An exceptionally clear and detailed coverage of western philosophy from the Renaissance to the end of the 19th century. Major and minor men such as Pomponazzi, Bodin, Boehme, Telesius, Bruno, Copernicus, da Vinci, Kepler, Galileo, Bacon, Descartes, Hobbes, Spinoza, Leibniz, Wolff, Locke, Newton, Berkeley, Hume, Erasmus, Montesquieu, Voltaire, Diderot, Rousseau, Lessing, Kant, Herder, Fichte, Schelling, Hegel, Schopenhauer, Comte, Mill, Darwin, Spencer, Hartmann, Lange, and many others, are discussed in terms of theory of knowledge, logic, cosmology, and psychology. Index. 2 volumes, total of 1159pp. 5⅜ x 8.
T117 Vol. 1, Paperbound **$2.25**
T118 Vol. 2, Paperbound **$2.25**

ARISTOTLE, A. E. Taylor. A brilliant, searching non-technical account of Aristotle and his thought written by a foremost Platonist. It covers the life and works of Aristotle; classification of the sciences; logic; first philosophy; matter and form; causes; motion and eternity; God; physics; metaphysics; and similar topics. Bibliography. New Index compiled for this edition. 128pp. 5⅜ x 8.
T280 Paperbound **$1.00**

THE SYSTEM OF THOMAS AQUINAS, M. de Wulf. Leading Neo-Thomist, one of founders of University of Louvain, gives concise exposition to central doctrines of Aquinas, as a means toward determining his value to modern philosophy, religion. Formerly "Medieval Philosophy Illustrated from the System of Thomas Aquinas." Trans. by E. Messenger. Introduction. 151pp. 5⅜ x 8.
T568 Paperbound **$1.25**

LEIBNIZ, H. W. Carr. Most stimulating middle-level coverage of basic philosophical thought of Leibniz. Easily understood discussion, analysis of major works: "Theodicy," "Principles of Nature and Grace," "Monadology"; Leibniz's influence; intellectual growth; correspondence; disputes with Bayle, Malebranche, Newton; importance of his thought today, with reinterpretation in modern terminology. "Power and mastery," London Times. Bibliography. Index. 226pp. 5⅜ x 8.
T624 Paperbound **$1.35**

CATALOGUE OF DOVER BOOKS

AN ESSAY CONCERNING HUMAN UNDERSTANDING, John Locke. Edited by A. C. Fraser. Unabridged reprinting of definitive edition; only complete edition of "Essay" in print. Marginal analyses of almost every paragraph; hundreds of footnotes; authoritative 140-page biographical, critical, historical prolegomena. Indexes. 1170pp. 5⅜ x 8.
T530 Vol. 1 (Books 1, 2) Paperbound **$2.25**
T531 Vol. 2 (Books 3, 4) Paperbound **$2.25**
2 volume set **$4.50**

THE PHILOSOPHY OF HISTORY, G. W. F. Hegel. One of the great classics of western thought which reveals Hegel's basic principle: that history is not chance but a rational process, the realization of the Spirit of Freedom. Ranges from the oriental cultures of subjective thought to the classical subjective cultures, to the modern absolute synthesis where spiritual and secular may be reconciled. Translation and introduction by J. Sibree. Introduction by C. Hegel. Special introduction for this edition by Prof. Carl Friedrich. xxxix + 447pp. 5⅜ x 8.
T112 Paperbound **$2.00**

THE PHILOSOPHY OF HEGEL, W. T. Stace. The first detailed analysis of Hegel's thought in English, this is especially valuable since so many of Hegel's works are out of print. Dr. Stace examines Hegel's debt to Greek idealists and the 18th century and then proceeds to a careful description and analysis of Hegel's first principles, categories, reason, dialectic method, his logic, philosophy of nature and spirit, etc. Index. Special 14 x 20 chart of Hegelian system. x + 526pp. 5⅜ x 8.
T254 Paperbound **$2.25**

THE WILL TO BELIEVE and HUMAN IMMORTALITY, W. James. Two complete books bound as one. THE WILL TO BELIEVE discusses the interrelations of belief, will, and intellect in man; chance vs. determinism, free will vs. determinism, free will vs. fate, pluralism vs. monism; the philosophies of Hegel and Spencer, and more. HUMAN IMMORTALITY examines the question of survival after death and develops an unusual and powerful argument for immortality. Two prefaces. Index. Total of 429pp. 5⅜ x 8.
T291 Paperbound **$2.45**

THE WORLD AND THE INDIVIDUAL, Josiah Royce. Only major effort by an American philosopher to interpret nature of things in systematic, comprehensive manner. Royce's formulation of an absolute voluntarism remains one of the original and profound solutions to the problems involved. Part One, Four Historical Conceptions of Being, inquires into first principles, true meaning and place of individuality. Part Two, Nature, Man, and the Moral Order, is application of first principles to problems concerning religion, evil, moral order. Introduction by J. E. Smith, Yale Univ. Index. 1070pp. 5⅜ x 8.
T561 Vol. 1 Paperbound **$2.75**
T562 Vol. 2 Paperbound **$2.75**
Two volume set **$5.50**

THE PHILOSOPHICAL WRITINGS OF PEIRCE, edited by J. Buchler. This book (formerly THE PHILOSOPHY OF PEIRCE) is a carefully integrated exposition of Peirce's complete system composed of selections from his own work. Symbolic logic, scientific method, theory of signs, pragmatism, epistemology, chance, cosmology, ethics, and many other topics are treated by one of the greatest philosophers of modern times. This is the only inexpensive compilation of his key ideas. xvi + 386pp. 5⅜ x 8.
T217 Paperbound **$2.00**

EXPERIENCE AND NATURE, John Dewey. An enlarged, revised edition of the Paul Carus lectures which Dewey delivered in 1925. It covers Dewey's basic formulation of the problem of knowledge, with a full discussion of other systems, and a detailing of his own concepts of the relationship of external world, mind, and knowledge. Starts with a thorough examination of the philosophical method; examines the interrelationship of experience and nature; analyzes experience on basis of empirical naturalism, the formulation of law, role of language and social factors in knowledge; etc. Dewey's treatment of central problems in philosophy is profound but extremely easy to follow. ix + 448pp. 5⅜ x 8.
T471 Paperbound **$2.00**

THE PHILOSOPHICAL WORKS OF DESCARTES. The definitive English edition of all the major philosophical works and letters of René Descartes. All of his revolutionary insights, from his famous "Cogito ergo sum" to his detailed account of contemporary science and his astonishingly fruitful concept that all phenomena of the universe (except mind) could be reduced to clear laws by the use of mathematics. An excellent source for the thought of men like Hobbes, Arnauld, Gassendi, etc., who were Descarte's contemporaries. Translated by E. S. Haldane and G. Ross. Introductory notes. Index. Total of 842pp. 5⅜ x 8.
T71 Vol. 1, Paperbound **$2.00**
T72 Vol. 2, Paperbound **$2.00**

THE CHIEF WORKS OF SPINOZA. An unabridged reprint of the famous Bohn edition containing all of Spinoza's most important works: Vol. I: The Theologico-Political Treatise and the Political Treatise. Vol. II: On The Improvement Of Understanding, The Ethics, Selected Letters. Profound and enduring ideas on God, the universe, pantheism, society, religion, the state, democracy, the mind, emotions, freedom and the nature of man, which influenced Goethe, Hegel, Schelling, Coleridge, Whitehead, and many others. Introduction. 2 volumes. 826pp. 5⅜ x 8.
T249 Vol. I, Paperbound **$1.50**
T250 Vol. II, Paperbound **$1.50**

CATALOGUE OF DOVER BOOKS

THE SENSE OF BEAUTY, G. Santayana. A revelation of the beauty of language as well as an important philosophic treatise, this work studies the "why, when, and how beauty appears, what conditions an object must fulfill to be beautiful, what elements of our nature make us sensible of beauty, and what the relation is between the constitution of the object and the excitement of our susceptibility." "It is doubtful if a better treatment of the subject has since been published," PEABODY JOURNAL. Index. ix + 275pp. 5⅜ x 8.
T238 Paperbound **$1.00**

PROBLEMS OF ETHICS, Moritz Schlick. The renowned leader of the "Vienna Circle" applies the logical positivist approach to a wide variety of ethical problems: the source and means of attaining knowledge, the formal and material characteristics of the good, moral norms and principles, absolute vs. relative values, free will and responsibility, comparative importance of pleasure and suffering as ethical values, etc. Disarmingly simple and straightforward despite complexity of subject. First English translation, authorized by author before his death, of a thirty-year old classic. Translated and with an introduction by David Rynin. Index. Foreword by Prof. George P. Adams. xxi + 209pp. 5⅜ x 8.
T946 Paperbound **$1.45**

AN INTRODUCTION TO EXISTENTIALISM, Robert G. Olson. A new and indispensable guide to one of the major thought systems of our century, the movement that is central to the thinking of some of the most creative figures of the past hundred years. Stresses Heidegger and Sartre, with careful and objective examination of the existentialist position, values—freedom of choice, individual dignity, personal love, creative effort—and answers to the eternal questions of the human condition. Scholarly, unbiased, analytic, unlike most studies of this difficult subject, Prof. Olson's book is aimed at the student of philosophy as well as at the reader with no formal training who is looking for an absorbing, accessible, and thorough introduction to the basic texts. Index. xv + 221pp. 5⅜ x 8½.
T55 Paperbound **$1.50**

SYMBOLIC LOGIC, C. I. Lewis and C. H. Langford. Since first publication in 1932, this has been among most frequently cited works on symbolic logic. Still one of the best introductions both for beginners and for mathematicians, philosophers. First part covers basic topics which easily lend themselves to beginning study. Second part is rigorous, thorough development of logistic method, examination of some of most difficult and abstract aspects of symbolic logic, including modal logic, logical paradoxes, many-valued logic, with Prof. Lewis' own contributions. 2nd revised (corrected) edition. 3 appendixes, one new to this edition. 524pp. 5⅜ x 8.
S170 Paperbound **$2.00**

WHITEHEAD'S PHILOSOPHY OF CIVILIZATION, A. H. Johnson. A leading authority on Alfred North Whitehead synthesizes the great philosopher's thought on civilization, scattered throughout various writings, into unified whole. Analysis of Whitehead's general definition of civilization, his reflections on history and influences on its development, his religion, including his analysis of Christianity, concept of solitariness as first requirement of personal religion, and so on. Other chapters cover views on minority groups, society, civil liberties, education. Also critical comments on Whitehead's philosophy. Written with general reader in mind. A perceptive introduction to important area of the thought of a leading philosopher of our century. Revised index and bibliography. xii + 211pp. 5⅜ x 8½.
T996 Paperbound **$1.50**

WHITEHEAD'S THEORY OF REALITY, A. H. Johnson. Introductory outline of Whitehead's theory of actual entities, the heart of his philosophy of reality, followed by his views on nature of God, philosophy of mind, theory of value (truth, beauty, goodness and their opposites), analyses of other philosophers, attitude toward science. A perspicacious lucid introduction by author of dissertation on Whitehead, written under the subject's supervision at Harvard. Good basic view for beginning students of philosophy and for those who are simply interested in important contemporary ideas. Revised index and bibliography. xiii + 267pp. 5⅜ x 8½.
T989 Paperbound **$1.50**

MIND AND THE WORLD-ORDER, C. I. Lewis. Building upon the work of Peirce, James, and Dewey, Professor Lewis outlines a theory of knowledge in terms of "conceptual pragmatism." Dividing truth into abstract mathematical certainty and empirical truth, the author demonstrates that the traditional understanding of the a priori must be abandoned. Detailed analyses of philosophy, metaphysics, method, the "given" in experience, knowledge of objects, nature of the a priori, experience and order, and many others. Appendices. xiv + 446pp. 5⅜ x 8.
T359 Paperbound **$2.25**

SCEPTICISM AND ANIMAL FAITH, G. Santayana. To eliminate difficulties in the traditional theory of knowledge, Santayana distinguishes between the independent existence of objects and the essence our mind attributes to them. Scepticism is thereby established as a form of belief, and animal faith is shown to be a necessary condition of knowledge. Belief, classical idealism, intuition, memory, symbols, literary psychology, and much more, discussed with unusual clarity and depth. Index. xii + 314pp. 5⅜ x 8.
T235 Clothbound **$3.50**
T236 Paperbound **$1.50**

LANGUAGE AND MYTH, E. Cassirer. Analyzing the non-rational thought processes which go to make up culture, Cassirer demonstrates that beneath both language and myth there lies a dominant unconscious "grammar" of experience whose categories and canons are not those of logical thought. His analyses of seemingly diverse phenomena such as Indian metaphysics, the Melanesian "mana," the Naturphilosophie of Schelling, modern poetry, etc., are profound without being pedantic. Introduction and translation by Susanne Langer. Index. x + 103pp. 5⅜ x 8.
T51 Paperbound **$1.25**

CATALOGUE OF DOVER BOOKS

THE ANALYSIS OF MATTER, Bertrand Russell. A classic which has retained its importance in understanding the relation between modern physical theory and human perception. Logical analysis of physics, prerelativity physics, causality, scientific inference, Weyl's theory, tensors, invariants and physical interpretations, periodicity, and much more is treated with Russell's usual brilliance. "Masterly piece of clear thinking and clear writing," NATION AND ATHENAEUM. "Most thorough treatment of the subject," THE NATION. Introduction. Index. 8 figures. viii + 408pp. 5⅜ x 8.   S231 Paperbound **$1.95**

CONCEPTUAL THINKING (A LOGICAL INQUIRY), S. Körner. Discusses origin, use of general concepts on which language is based, and the light they shed on basic philosophical questions. Rigorously examines how different concepts are related; how they are linked to experience; problems in the field of contact between exact logical, mathematical, and scientific concepts, and the inexactness of everyday experience (studied at length). This work elaborates many new approaches to the traditional problems of philosophy—epistemology, value theories, metaphysics, aesthetics, morality. "Rare originality . . . brings a new rigour into philosophical argument," Philosophical Quarterly. New corrected second edition. Index. vii + 301pp. 5⅜ x 8.   T516 Paperbound **$1.75**

INTRODUCTION TO SYMBOLIC LOGIC, S. Langer. No special knowledge of math required — probably the clearest book ever written on symbolic logic, suitable for the layman, general scientist, and philosopher. You start with simple symbols and advance to a knowledge of the Boole-Schroeder and Russell-Whitehead systems. Forms, logical structure, classes, the calculus of propositions, logic of the syllogism, etc., are all covered. "One of the clearest and simplest introductions," MATHEMATICS GAZETTE. Second enlarged, revised edition. 368pp. 5⅜ x 8.   S164 Paperbound **$1.75**

LANGUAGE, TRUTH AND LOGIC, A. J. Ayer. A clear, careful analysis of the basic ideas of Logical Positivism. Building on the work of Schlick, Russell, Carnap, and the Viennese School, Mr. Ayer develops a detailed exposition of the nature of philosophy, science, and metaphysics; the Self and the World; logic and common sense, and other philosophic concepts. An aid to clarity of thought as well as the first full-length development of Logical Positivism in English. Introduction by Bertrand Russell. Index. 160pp. 5⅜ x 8.   T10 Paperbound **$1.25**

ESSAYS IN EXPERIMENTAL LOGIC, J. Dewey. Based upon the theory that knowledge implies a judgment which in turn implies an inquiry, these papers consider the inquiry stage in terms of: the relationship of thought and subject matter, antecedents of thought, data and meanings. 3 papers examine Bertrand Russell's thought, while 2 others discuss pragmatism and a final essay presents a new theory of the logic of values. Index. viii + 444pp. 5⅜ x 8.
                                                                      T73 Paperbound **$1.95**

TRAGIC SENSE OF LIFE, M. de Unamuno. The acknowledged masterpiece of one of Spain's most influential thinkers. Between the despair at the inevitable death of man and all his works and the desire for something better, Unamuno finds that "saving incertitude" that alone can console us. This dynamic appraisal of man's faith in God and in himself has been called "a masterpiece" by the ENCYCLOPAEDIA BRITANNICA. xxx + 332pp. 5⅜ x 8.
                                                                      T257 Paperbound **$2.00**

HISTORY OF DOGMA, A. Harnack. Adolph Harnack, who died in 1930, was perhaps the greatest Church historian of all time. In this epoch-making history, which has never been surpassed in comprehensiveness and wealth of learning, he traces the development of the authoritative Christian doctrinal system from its first crystallization in the 4th century down through the Reformation, including also a brief survey of the later developments through the Infallibility decree of 1870. He reveals the enormous influence of Greek thought on the early Fathers, and discusses such topics as the Apologists, the great councils, Manichaeism, the historical position of Augustine, the medieval opposition to indulgences, the rise of Protestantism, the relations of Luther's doctrines with modern tendencies of thought, and much more. "Monumental work; still the most valuable history of dogma . . . luminous analysis of the problems . . . abounds in suggestion and stimulus and can be neglected by no one who desires to understand the history of thought in this most important field," Dutcher's Guide to Historical Literature. Translated by Neil Buchanan. Index. Unabridged reprint in 4 volumes. Vol I: Beginnings to the Gnostics and Marcion. Vol II & III: 2nd century to the 4th century Fathers. Vol IV & V: 4th century Councils to the Carlovingian Renaissance. Vol VI & VII: Period of Clugny (c. 1000) to the Reformation, and after. Total of cii + 2407pp. 5⅜ x 8.

T904 Vol I	Paperbound	**$2.50**
T905 Vol II & III	Paperbound	**$2.50**
T906 Vol IV & V	Paperbound	**$2.50**
T907 Vol VI & VII	Paperbound	**$2.50**
	The set	**$10.00**

THE GUIDE FOR THE PERPLEXED, Maimonides. One of the great philosophical works of all time and a necessity for everyone interested in the philosophy of the Middle Ages in the Jewish, Christian, and Moslem traditions. Maimonides develops a common meeting-point for the Old Testament and the Aristotelian thought which pervaded the medieval world. His ideas and methods predate such scholastics as Aquinas and Scotus and throw light on the entire problem of philosophy or science vs. religion. 2nd revised edition. Complete unabridged Friedländer translation. 55 page introduction to Maimonides's life, period, etc., with an important summary of the GUIDE. Index. lix + 414pp. 5⅜ x 8.   T351 Paperbound **$2.00**

CATALOGUE OF DOVER BOOKS

Americana

THE EYES OF DISCOVERY, J. Bakeless. A vivid reconstruction of how unspoiled America appeared to the first white men. Authentic and enlightening accounts of Hudson's landing in New York, Coronado's trek through the Southwest; scores of explorers, settlers, trappers, soldiers. America's pristine flora, fauna, and Indians in every region and state in fresh and unusual new aspects. "A fascinating view of what the land was like before the first highway went through," Time. 68 contemporary illustrations, 39 newly added in this edition. Index. Bibliography. x + 500pp. 5⅜ x 8.   T761 Paperbound **$2.00**

AUDUBON AND HIS JOURNALS, J. J. Audubon. A collection of fascinating accounts of Europe and America in the early 1800's through Audubon's own eyes. Includes the Missouri River Journals —an eventful trip through America's untouched heartland, the Labrador Journals, the European Journals, the famous "Episodes", and other rare Audubon material, including the descriptive chapters from the original letterpress edition of the "Ornithological Studies", omitted in all later editions. Indispensable for ornithologists, naturalists, and all lovers of Americana and adventure. 70-page biography by Audubon's granddaughter. 38 illustrations. Index. Total of 1106pp. 5⅜ x 8.   T675 Vol I Paperbound **$2.25**
T676 Vol II Paperbound **$2.25**
The set **$4.50**

TRAVELS OF WILLIAM BARTRAM, edited by Mark Van Doren. The first inexpensive illustrated edition of one of the 18th century's most delightful books is an excellent source of first-hand material on American geography, anthropology, and natural history. Many descriptions of early Indian tribes are our only source of information on them prior to the infiltration of the white man. "The mind of a scientist with the soul of a poet," John Livingston Lowes. 13 original illustrations and maps. Edited with an introduction by Mark Van Doren. 448pp. 5⅜ x 8.
T13 Paperbound **$2.00**

GARRETS AND PRETENDERS: A HISTORY OF BOHEMIANISM IN AMERICA, A. Parry. The colorful and fantastic history of American Bohemianism from Poe to Kerouac. This is the only complete record of hoboes, cranks, starving poets, and suicides. Here are Pfaff, Whitman, Crane, Bierce, Pound, and many others. New chapters by the author and by H. T. Moore bring this thorough and well-documented history down to the Beatniks. "An excellent account," N. Y. Times. Scores of cartoons, drawings, and caricatures. Bibliography. Index. xxviii + 421pp. 5⅝ x 8⅜.   T708 Paperbound **$1.95**

THE EXPLORATION OF THE COLORADO RIVER AND ITS CANYONS, J. W. Powell. The thrilling first-hand account of the expedition that filled in the last white space on the map of the United States. Rapids, famine, hostile Indians, and mutiny are among the perils encountered as the unknown Colorado Valley reveals its secrets. This is the only uncut version of Major Powell's classic of exploration that has been printed in the last 60 years. Includes later reflections and subsequent expedition. 250 illustrations, new map. 400pp. 5⅝ x 8⅜.
T94 Paperbound **$2.00**

THE JOURNAL OF HENRY D. THOREAU, Edited by Bradford Torrey and Francis H. Allen. Henry Thoreau is not only one of the most important figures in American literature and social thought; his voluminous journals (from which his books emerged as selections and crystallizations) constitute both the longest, most sensitive record of personal internal development and a most penetrating description of a historical moment in American culture. This present set, which was first issued in fourteen volumes, contains Thoreau's entire journals from 1837 to 1862, with the exception of the lost years which were found only recently. We are reissuing it, complete and unabridged, with a new introduction by Walter Harding, Secretary of the Thoreau Society. Fourteen volumes reissued in two volumes. Foreword by Henry Seidel Canby. Total of 1888pp. 8⅜ x 12¼.   T312-3 Two volume set, Clothbound **$20.00**

GAMES AND SONGS OF AMERICAN CHILDREN, collected by William Wells Newell. A remarkable collection of 190 games with songs that accompany many of them; cross references to show similarities, differences among them; variations; musical notation for 38 songs. Textual discussions show relations with folk-drama and other aspects of folk tradition. Grouped into categories for ready comparative study: Love-games, histories, playing at work, human life, bird and beast, mythology, guessing-games, etc. New introduction covers relations of songs and dances to timeless heritage of folklore, biographical sketch of Newell, other pertinent data. A good source of inspiration for those in charge of groups of children and a valuable reference for anthropologists, sociologists, psychiatrists. Introduction by Carl Withers. New indexes of first lines, games. 5⅜ x 8½. xii + 242pp.   T354 Paperbound **$1.75**

CATALOGUE OF DOVER BOOKS

GARDNER'S PHOTOGRAPHIC SKETCH BOOK OF THE CIVIL WAR, Alexander Gardner. The first published collection of Civil War photographs, by one of the two or three most famous photographers of the era, outstandingly reproduced from the original positives. Scenes of crucial battles: Appomattox, Manassas, Mechanicsville, Bull Run, Yorktown, Fredericksburg, etc. Gettysburg immediately after retirement of forces. Battle ruins at Richmond, Petersburg, Gaines'Mill. Prisons, arsenals, a slave pen, fortifications, headquarters, pontoon bridges, soldiers, a field hospital. A unique glimpse into the realities of one of the bloodiest wars in history, with an introductory text to each picture by Gardner himself. Until this edition, there were only five known copies in libraries, and fewer in private hands, one of which sold at auction in 1952 for $425. Introduction by E. F. Bleiler. 100 full page 7 x 10 photographs (original size). 224pp. 8½ x 10¾.   T476 Clothbound **$6.00**

A BIBLIOGRAPHY OF NORTH AMERICAN FOLKLORE AND FOLKSONG, Charles Haywood, Ph.D. The only book that brings together bibliographic information on so wide a range of folklore material. Lists practically everything published about American folksongs, ballads, dances, folk beliefs and practices, popular music, tales, similar material—more than 35,000 titles of books, articles, periodicals, monographs, music publications, phonograph records. Each entry complete with author, title, date and place of publication, arranger and performer of particular examples of folk music, many with Dr. Haywood's valuable criticism, evaluation. Volume I, "The American People," is complete listing of general and regional studies, titles of tales and songs of Negro and non-English speaking groups and where to find them, Occupational Bibliography including sections listing sources of information, folk material on cowboys, riverboat men, 49ers, American characters like Mike Fink, Frankie and Johnnie, John Henry, many more. Volume II, "The American Indian," tells where to find information on dances, myths, songs, ritual of more than 250 tribes in U.S., Canada. A monumental product of 10 years' labor, carefully classified for easy use. "All students of this subject . . . will find themselves in debt to Professor Haywood," Stith Thompson, in American Anthropologist. ". . . a most useful and excellent work," Duncan Emrich, Chief Folklore Section, Library of Congress, in "Notes." Corrected, enlarged republication of 1951 edition. New Preface. New index of composers, arrangers, performers. General index of more than 15,000 items. Two volumes. Total of 1301pp. 6⅛ x 9¼.   T797-798 Clothbound **$12.50**

INCIDENTS OF TRAVEL IN YUCATAN, John L. Stephens. One of first white men to penetrate interior of Yucatan tells the thrilling story of his discoveries of 44 cities, remains of once-powerful Maya civilization. Compelling text combines narrative power with historical significance as it takes you through heat, dust, storms of Yucatan; native festivals with brutal bull fights; great ruined temples atop man-made mounds. Countless idols, sculptures, tombs, examples of Mayan taste for rich ornamentation, from gateways to personal trinkets, accurately illustrated, discussed in text. Will appeal to those interested in ancient civilizations, and those who like stories of exploration, discovery, adventure. Republication of last (1843) edition. 124 illustrations by English artist, F. Catherwood. Appendix on Mayan architecture, chronology. Two volume set. Total of xxviii + 927pp.

Vol I T926 Paperbound **$2.00**
Vol II T927 Paperbound **$2.00**
The set **$4.00**

A GENIUS IN THE FAMILY, Hiram Percy Maxim. Sir Hiram Stevens Maxim was known to the public as the inventive genius who created the Maxim gun, automatic sprinkler, and a heavier-than-air plane that got off the ground in 1894. Here, his son reminisces—this is by no means a formal biography—about the exciting and often downright scandalous private life of his brilliant, eccentric father. A warm and winning portrait of a prankish, mischievous, impious personality, a genuine character. The style is fresh and direct, the effect is unadulterated pleasure. "A book of charm and lasting humor . . . belongs on the 'must read' list of all fathers," New York Times. "A truly gorgeous affair," New Statesman and Nation. 17 illustrations, 16 specially for this edition. viii + 108pp. 5⅜ x 8½.   T948 Paperbound **$1.00**

HORSELESS CARRIAGE DAYS, Hiram P. Maxim. The best account of an important technological revolution by one of its leading figures. The delightful and rewarding story of the author's experiments with the exact combustibility of gasoline, stopping and starting mechanisms, carriage design, and engines. Captures remarkably well the flavor of an age of scoffers and rival inventors not above sabotage; of noisy, uncontrollable gasoline vehicles and incredible mobile steam kettles. ". . . historic information and light humor are combined to furnish highly entertaining reading," New York Times. 56 photographs, 12 specially for this edition. xi + 175pp. 5⅜ x 8½.   T964 Paperbound **$1.35**

BODY, BOOTS AND BRITCHES: FOLKTALES, BALLADS AND SPEECH FROM COUNTRY NEW YORK, Harold W. Thompson. A unique collection, discussion of songs, stories, anecdotes, proverbs handed down orally from Scotch-Irish grandfathers, German nurse-maids, Negro workmen, gathered from all over Upper New York State. Tall tales by and about lumbermen and pirates, canalers and injun-fighters, tragic and comic ballads, scores of sayings and proverbs all tied together by an informative, delightful narrative by former president of New York Historical Society. ". . . a sparkling homespun tapestry that every lover of Americana will want to have around the house," Carl Carmer, New York Times. Republication of 1939 edition. 20 line-drawings. Index. Appendix (Sources of material, bibliography). 530pp. 5⅜ x 8½.   T411 Paperbound **$2.00**

Puzzles, Mathematical Recreations

SYMBOLIC LOGIC and THE GAME OF LOGIC, Lewis Carroll. "Symbolic Logic" is not concerned with modern symbolic logic, but is instead a collection of over 380 problems posed with charm and imagination, using the syllogism, and a fascinating diagrammatic method of drawing conclusions. In "The Game of Logic" Carroll's whimsical imagination devises a logical game played with 2 diagrams and counters (included) to manipulate hundreds of tricky syllogisms. The final section, "Hit or Miss" is a lagniappe of 101 additional puzzles in the delightful Carroll manner. Until this reprint edition, both of these books were rarities costing up to $15 each. Symbolic Logic: Index. xxxi + 199pp. The Game of Logic: 96pp. 2 vols. bound as one. 5⅜ x 8. **T492 Paperbound $1.50**

PILLOW PROBLEMS and A TANGLED TALE, Lewis Carroll. One of the rarest of all Carroll's works, "Pillow Problems" contains 72 original math puzzles, all typically ingenious. Particularly fascinating are Carroll's answers which remain exactly as he thought them out, reflecting his actual mental process. The problems in "A Tangled Tale" are in story form, originally appearing as a monthly magazine serial. Carroll not only gives the solutions, but uses answers sent in by readers to discuss wrong approaches and misleading paths, and grades them for insight. Both of these books were rarities until this edition, "Pillow Problems" costing up to $25, and "A Tangled Tale" $15. Pillow Problems: Preface and Introduction by Lewis Carroll. xx + 109pp. A Tangled Tale: 6 illustrations. 152pp. Two vols. bound as one. 5⅜ x 8. **T493 Paperbound $1.50**

AMUSEMENTS IN MATHEMATICS, Henry Ernest Dudeney. The foremost British originator of mathematical puzzles is always intriguing, witty, and paradoxical in this classic, one of the largest collections of mathematical amusements. More than 430 puzzles, problems, and paradoxes. Mazes and games, problems on number manipulation, unicursal and other route problems, puzzles on measuring, weighing, packing, age, kinship, chessboards, joiners', crossing river, plane figure dissection, and many others. Solutions. More than 450 illustrations. vii + 258pp. 5⅜ x 8. **T473 Paperbound $1.25**

THE CANTERBURY PUZZLES, Henry Dudeney. Chaucer's pilgrims set one another problems in story form. Also Adventures of the Puzzle Club, the Strange Escape of the King's Jester, the Monks of Riddlewell, the Squire's Christmas Puzzle Party, and others. All puzzles are original, based on dissecting plane figures, arithmetic, algebra, elementary calculus and other branches of mathematics, and purely logical ingenuity. "The limit of ingenuity and intricacy," The Observer. Over 110 puzzles. Full Solutions. 150 illustrations. vii + 225pp. 5⅜ x 8. **T474 Paperbound $1.25**

MATHEMATICAL EXCURSIONS, H. A. Merrill. Even if you hardly remember your high school math, you'll enjoy the 90 stimulating problems contained in this book and you will come to understand a great many mathematical principles with surprisingly little effort. Many useful shortcuts and diversions not generally known are included: division by inspection, Russian peasant multiplication, memory systems for pi, building odd and even magic squares, square roots by geometry, dyadic systems, and many more. Solutions to difficult problems. 50 illustrations. 145pp. 5⅜ x 8. **T350 Paperbound $1.00**

MAGIC SQUARES AND CUBES, W. S. Andrews. Only book-length treatment in English, a thorough non-technical description and analysis. Here are nasik, overlapping, pandiagonal, serrated squares; magic circles, cubes, spheres, rhombuses. Try your hand at 4-dimensional magical figures! Much unusual folklore and tradition included. High school algebra is sufficient. 754 diagrams and illustrations. viii + 419pp. 5⅜ x 8. **T658 Paperbound $1.85**

CALIBAN'S PROBLEM BOOK: MATHEMATICAL, INFERENTIAL AND CRYPTOGRAPHIC PUZZLES, H. Phillips (Caliban); S. T. Shovelton, G. S. Marshall. 105 ingenious problems by the greatest living creator of puzzles based on logic and inference. Rigorous, modern, piquant; reflecting their author's unusual personality, these intermediate and advanced puzzles all involve the ability to reason clearly through complex situations; some call for mathematical knowledge, ranging from algebra to number theory. Solutions. xi + 180pp. 5⅜ x 8. **T736 Paperbound $1.25**

MATHEMATICAL PUZZLES FOR BEGINNERS AND ENTHUSIASTS, G. Mott-Smith. 188 mathematical puzzles based on algebra, dissection of plane figures, permutations, and probability, that will test and improve your powers of inference and interpretation. The Odic Force, The Spider's Cousin, Ellipse Drawing, theory and strategy of card and board games like tit-tat-toe, go moku, salvo, and many others. 100 pages of detailed mathematical explanations. Appendix of primes, square roots, etc. 135 illustrations. 2nd revised edition. 248pp. 5⅜ x 8. **T198 Paperbound $1.00**

MATHEMAGIC, MAGIC PUZZLES, AND GAMES WITH NUMBERS, R. V. Heath. More than 60 new puzzles and stunts based on the properties of numbers. Easy techniques for multiplying large numbers mentally, revealing hidden numbers magically, finding the date of any day in any year, and dozens more. Over 30 pages devoted to magic squares, triangles, cubes, circles, etc. Edited by J. S. Meyer. 76 illustrations. 128pp. 5⅜ x 8. **T110 Paperbound $1.00**

CATALOGUE OF DOVER BOOKS

MATHEMATICAL RECREATIONS, M. Kraitchik. One of the most thorough compilations of unusual mathematical problems for beginners and advanced mathematicians. Historical problems from Greek, Medieval, Arabic, Hindu sources. 50 pages devoted to pastimes derived from figurate numbers, Mersenne numbers, Fermat numbers, primes and probability. 40 pages of magic, Euler, Latin, panmagic squares. 25 new positional and permutational games of permanent value: fairy chess, latruncles, reversi, jinx, ruma, lasca, tricolor, tetrachrome, etc. Complete rigorous solutions. Revised second edition. 181 illustrations. 333pp. 5⅜ x 8.
T163 Paperbound **$1.75**

MATHEMATICAL PUZZLES OF SAM LOYD, selected and edited by M. Gardner. Choice puzzles by the greatest American puzzle creator and innovator. Selected from his famous collection, "Cyclopedia of Puzzles," they retain the unique style and historical flavor of the originals. There are posers based on arithmetic, algebra, probability, game theory, route tracing, topology, counter, sliding block, operations research, geometrical dissection. Includes the famous "14-15" puzzle which was a national craze, and his "Horse of a Different Color" which sold millions of copies. 117 of his most ingenious puzzles in all, 120 line drawings and diagrams. Solutions. Selected references. xx + 167pp. 5⅜ x 8. T498 Paperbound **$1.00**

MATHEMATICAL PUZZLES OF SAM LOYD, Vol. II, selected and edited by Martin Gardner. The outstanding 2nd selection from the great American innovator's "Cyclopedia of Puzzles": speed and distance problems, clock problems, plane and solid geometry, calculus problems, etc. Analytical table of contents that groups the puzzles according to the type of mathematics necessary to solve them. 166 puzzles, 150 original line drawings and diagrams. Selected references. xiv + 177pp. 5⅜ x 8. T709 Paperbound **$1.00**

ARITHMETICAL EXCURSIONS: AN ENRICHMENT OF ELEMENTARY MATHEMATICS, H. Bowers and J. Bowers. A lively and lighthearted collection of facts and entertainments for anyone who enjoys manipulating numbers or solving arithmetical puzzles: methods of arithmetic never taught in school, little-known facts about the most simple numbers, and clear explanations of more sophisticated topics; mysteries and folklore of numbers, the "Hin-dog-abic" number system, etc. First publication. Index. 529 numbered problems and diversions, all with answers. Bibliography. 60 figures. xiv + 320pp. 5⅜ x 8. T770 Paperbound **$1.65**

CRYPTANALYSIS, H. F. Gaines. Formerly entitled ELEMENTARY CRYPTANALYSIS, this introductory-intermediate level text is the best book in print on cryptograms and their solution. It covers all major techniques of the past, and contains much that is not generally known except to experts. Full details about concealment, substitution, and transposition ciphers; periodic mixed alphabets, multafid, Kasiski and Vigenere methods, Ohaver patterns, Playfair, and scores of other topics. 6 language letter and word frequency appendix. 167 problems, now furnished with solutions. Index. 173 figures. vi + 230pp. 5⅜ x 8.
T97 Paperbound **$2.00**

CRYPTOGRAPHY, L. D. Smith. An excellent introductory work on ciphers and their solution, the history of secret writing, and actual methods and problems in such techniques as transposition and substitution. Appendices describe the enciphering of Japanese, the Baconian biliteral cipher, and contain frequency tables and a bibliography for further study. Over 150 problems with solutions. 160pp. 5⅜ x 8. T247 Paperbound **$1.00**

PUZZLE QUIZ AND STUNT FUN, J. Meyer. The solution to party doldrums. 238 challenging puzzles, stunts and tricks. Mathematical puzzles like The Clever Carpenter, Atom Bomb; mysteries and deductions like The Bridge of Sighs, The Nine Pearls, Dog Logic; observation puzzles like Cigarette Smokers, Telephone Dial; over 200 others including magic squares, tongue twisters, puns, anagrams, and many others. All problems solved fully. 250pp. 5⅜ x 8.
T337 Paperbound **$1.00**

101 PUZZLES IN THOUGHT AND LOGIC, C. R. Wylie, Jr. Brand new problems you need no special knowledge to solve! Take the kinks out of your mental "muscles" and enjoy solving murder problems, the detection of lying fishermen, the logical identification of color by a blindman, and dozens more. Introduction with simplified explanation of general scientific method and puzzle solving. 128pp. 5⅜ x 8. T367 Paperbound **$1.00**

MY BEST PROBLEMS IN MATHEMATICS, Hubert Phillips ("Caliban"). Only elementary mathematics needed to solve these 100 witty, catchy problems by a master problem creator. Problems on the odds in cards and dice, problems in geometry, algebra, permutations, even problems that require no math at all—just a logical mind, clear thinking. Solutions completely worked out. If you enjoy mysteries, alerting your perceptive powers and exercising your detective's eye, you'll find these cryptic puzzles a challenging delight. Original 1961 publication. 100 puzzles, solutions. x + 107pp. 5⅝ x 8. T91 Paperbound **$1.00**

MY BEST PUZZLES IN LOGIC AND REASONING, Hubert Phillips ("Caliban"). A new collection of 100 inferential and logical puzzles chosen from the best that have appeared in England, available for first time in U.S. By the most endlessly resourceful puzzle creator now living. All data presented are both necessary and sufficient to allow a single unambiguous answer. No special knowledge is required for problems ranging from relatively simple to completely original one-of-a-kinds. Guaranteed to please beginners and experts of all ages. Original publication. 100 puzzles, full solutions. x + 107pp. 5⅜ x 8. T119 Paperbound **$1.00**

CATALOGUE OF DOVER BOOKS

THE BOOK OF MODERN PUZZLES, G. L. Kaufman. A completely new series of puzzles as fascinating as crossword and deduction puzzles but based upon different principles and techniques. Simple 2-minute teasers, word labyrinths, design and pattern puzzles, logic and observation puzzles — over 150 braincrackers. Answers to all problems. 116 illustrations. 192pp. 5⅜ x 8.
T143 Paperbound **$1.00**

NEW WORD PUZZLES, G. L. Kaufman. 100 ENTIRELY NEW puzzles based on words and their combinations that will delight crossword puzzle, Scrabble and Jotto fans. Chess words, based on the moves of the chess king; design-onyms, symmetrical designs made of synonyms; rhymed double-crostics; syllable sentences; addle letter anagrams; alphagrams; linkograms; and many others all brand new. Full solutions. Space to work problems. 196 figures. vi + 122pp. 5⅜ x 8.
T344 Paperbound **$1.00**

MAZES AND LABYRINTHS: A BOOK OF PUZZLES, W. Shepherd. Mazes, formerly associated with mystery and ritual, are still among the most intriguing of intellectual puzzles. This is a novel and different collection of 50 amusements that embody the principle of the maze: mazes in the classical tradition; 3-dimensional, ribbon, and Möbius-strip mazes; hidden messages; spatial arrangements; etc.—almost all built on amusing story situations. 84 illustrations. Essay on maze psychology. Solutions. xv + 122pp. 5⅜ x 8.
T731 Paperbound **$1.00**

MAGIC TRICKS & CARD TRICKS, W. Jonson. Two books bound as one. 52 tricks with cards, 37 tricks with coins, bills, eggs, smoke, ribbons, slates, etc. Details on presentation, misdirection, and routining will help you master such famous tricks as the Changing Card, Card in the Pocket, Four Aces, Coin Through the Hand, Bill in the Egg, Afghan Bands, and over 75 others. If you follow the lucid exposition and key diagrams carefully, you will finish these two books with an astonishing mastery of magic. 106 figures. 224pp. 5⅜ x 8. T909 Paperbound **$1.00**

PANORAMA OF MAGIC, Milbourne Christopher. A profusely illustrated history of stage magic, a unique selection of prints and engravings from the author's private collection of magic memorabilia, the largest of its kind. Apparatus, stage settings and costumes; ingenious ads distributed by the performers and satiric broadsides passed around in the streets ridiculing pompous showmen; programs; decorative souvenirs. The lively text, by one of America's foremost professional magicians, is full of anecdotes about almost legendary wizards: Dede, the Egyptian; Philadelphia, the wonder-worker; Robert-Houdin, "the father of modern magic;" Harry Houdini; scores more. Altogether a pleasure package for anyone interested in magic, stage setting and design, ethnology, psychology, or simply in unusual people. A Dover original. 295 illustrations; 8 in full color. Index. viii + 216pp. 8⅜ x 11¼.
T774 Paperbound **$2.25**

HOUDINI ON MAGIC, Harry Houdini. One of the greatest magicians of modern times explains his most prized secrets. How locks are picked, with illustrated picks and skeleton keys; how a girl is sawed into twins; how to walk through a brick wall — Houdini's explanations of 44 stage tricks with many diagrams. Also included is a fascinating discussion of great magicians of the past and the story of his fight against fraudulent mediums and spiritualists. Edited by W.B. Gibson and M.N. Young. Bibliography. 155 figures, photos. xv + 280pp. 5⅜ x 8.
T384 Paperbound **$1.25**

MATHEMATICS, MAGIC AND MYSTERY, Martin Gardner. Why do card tricks work? How do magicians perform astonishing mathematical feats? How is stage mind-reading possible? This is the first book length study explaining the application of probability, set theory, theory of numbers, topology, etc., to achieve many startling tricks. Non-technical, accurate, detailed! 115 sections discuss tricks with cards, dice, coins, knots, geometrical vanishing illusions, how a Curry square "demonstrates" that the sum of the parts may be greater than the whole, and dozens of others. No sleight of hand necessary! 135 illustrations. xii + 174pp. 5⅜ x 8.
T335 Paperbound **$1.00**

EASY-TO-DO ENTERTAINMENTS AND DIVERSIONS WITH COINS, CARDS, STRING, PAPER AND MATCHES, R. M. Abraham. Over 300 tricks, games and puzzles will provide young readers with absorbing fun. Sections on card games; paper-folding; tricks with coins, matches and pieces of string; games for the agile; toy-making from common household objects; mathematical recreations; and 50 miscellaneous pastimes. Anyone in charge of groups of youngsters, including hard-pressed parents, and in need of suggestions on how to keep children sensibly amused and quietly content will find this book indispensable. Clear, simple text, copious number of delightful line drawings and illustrative diagrams. Originally titled "Winter Nights Entertainments." Introduction by Lord Baden Powell. 329 illustrations. v + 186pp. 5⅜ x 8½.
T921 Paperbound **$1.00**

STRING FIGURES AND HOW TO MAKE THEM, Caroline Furness Jayne. 107 string figures plus variations selected from the best primitive and modern examples developed by Navajo, Apache, pygmies of Africa, Eskimo, in Europe, Australia, China, etc. The most readily understandable, easy-to-follow book in English on perennially popular recreation. Crystal-clear exposition; step-by-step diagrams. Everyone from kindergarten children to adults looking for unusual diversion will be endlessly amused. Index. Bibliography. Introduction by A. C. Haddon. 17 full-page plates. 960 illustrations. xxiii + 401pp. 5⅜ x 8½.
T152 Paperbound **$2.00**

Entertainments, Humor

ODDITIES AND CURIOSITIES OF WORDS AND LITERATURE, C. Bombaugh, edited by M. Gardner. The largest collection of idiosyncratic prose and poetry techniques in English, a legendary work in the curious and amusing bypaths of literary recreations and the play technique in literature—so important in modern works. Contains alphabetic poetry, acrostics, palindromes, scissors verse, centos, emblematic poetry, famous literary puns, hoaxes, notorious slips of the press, hilarious mistranslations, and much more. Revised and enlarged with modern material by Martin Gardner. 368pp. 5⅜ x 8. T759 Paperbound **$1.50**

A NONSENSE ANTHOLOGY, collected by Carolyn Wells. 245 of the best nonsense verses ever written, including nonsense puns, absurd arguments, mock epics and sagas, nonsense ballads, odes, "sick" verses, dog-Latin verses, French nonsense verses, songs. By Edward Lear, Lewis Carroll, Gelett Burgess, W. S. Gilbert, Hilaire Belloc, Peter Newell, Oliver Herford, etc., 83 writers in all plus over four score anonymous nonsense verses. A special section of limericks, plus famous nonsense such as Carroll's "Jabberwocky" and Lear's "The Jumblies" and much excellent verse virtually impossible to locate elsewhere. For 50 years considered the best anthology available. Index of first lines specially prepared for this edition. Introduction by Carolyn Wells. 3 indexes: Title, Author, First lines. xxxiii + 279pp. T499 Paperbound **$1.35**

THE BAD CHILD'S BOOK OF BEASTS, MORE BEASTS FOR WORSE CHILDREN, and A MORAL ALPHA-BET, H. Belloc. Hardly an anthology of humorous verse has appeared in the last 50 years without at least a couple of these famous nonsense verses. But one must see the entire volumes—with all the delightful original illustrations by Sir Basil Blackwood—to appreciate fully Belloc's charming and witty verses that play so subacidly on the platitudes of life and morals that beset his day—and ours. A great humor classic. Three books in one. Total of 157pp. 5⅜ x 8. T749 Paperbound **$1.00**

THE DEVIL'S DICTIONARY, Ambrose Bierce. Sardonic and irreverent barbs puncturing the pomposities and absurdities of American politics, business, religion, literature, and arts, by the country's greatest satirist in the classic tradition. Epigrammatic as Shaw, piercing as Swift, American as Mark Twain, Will Rogers, and Fred Allen, Bierce will always remain the favorite of a small coterie of enthusiasts, and of writers and speakers whom he supplies with "some of the most gorgeous witticisms of the English language" (H. L. Mencken). Over 1000 entries in alphabetical order. 144pp. 5⅜ x 8. T487 Paperbound **$1.00**

THE PURPLE COW AND OTHER NONSENSE, Gelett Burgess. The best of Burgess's early nonsense, selected from the first edition of the "Burgess Nonsense Book." Contains many of his most unusual and truly awe-inspiring pieces: 36 nonsense quatrains, the Poems of Patagonia, Alphabet of Famous Goops, and the other hilarious (and rare) adult nonsense that place him in the forefront of American humorists. All pieces are accompanied by the original Burgess illustrations. 123 illustrations. xiii + 113pp. 5⅜ x 8. T772 Paperbound **$1.00**

MY PIOUS FRIENDS AND DRUNKEN COMPANIONS and MORE PIOUS FRIENDS AND DRUNKEN COMPANIONS, Frank Shay. Folksingers, amateur and professional, and everyone who loves singing: here, available for the first time in 30 years, is this valued collection of 132 ballads, blues, vaudeville numbers, drinking songs, sea chanties, comedy songs. Songs of pre-Beatnik Bohemia; songs from all over America, England, France, Australia; the great songs of the Naughty Nineties and early twentieth-century America. Over a third with music. Woodcuts by John Held, Jr. convey perfectly the brash insouciance of an era of rollicking unabashed song. 12 illustrations by John Held, Jr. Two indexes (Titles and First lines and Choruses). Introductions by the author. Two volumes bound as one. Total of xvi + 235pp. 5⅜ x 8½. T946 Paperbound **$1.25**

HOW TO TELL THE BIRDS FROM THE FLOWERS, R. W. Wood. How not to confuse a carrot with a parrot, a grape with an ape, a puffin with nuffin. Delightful drawings, clever puns, absurd little poems point out far-fetched resemblances in nature. The author was a leading physicist. Introduction by Margaret Wood White. 106 illus. 60pp. 5⅜ x 8. T523 Paperbound **75¢**

PECK'S BAD BOY AND HIS PA, George W. Peck. The complete edition, containing both volumes, of one of the most widely read American humor books. The endless ingenious pranks played by bad boy "Hennery" on his pa and the grocery man, the outraged pomposity of Pa, the perpetual ridiculing of middle class institutions, are as entertaining today as they were in 1883. No pale sophistications or subtleties, but rather humor vigorous, raw, earthy, imaginative, and, as folk humor often is, sadistic. This peculiarly fascinating book is also valuable to historians and students of American culture as a portrait of an age. 100 original illustrations by True Williams. Introduction by E. F. Bleiler. 347pp. 5⅜ x 8. T497 Paperbound **$1.35**

CATALOGUE OF DOVER BOOKS

THE HUMOROUS VERSE OF LEWIS CARROLL. Almost every poem Carroll ever wrote, the largest collection ever published, including much never published elsewhere: 150 parodies, burlesques, riddles, ballads, acrostics, etc., with 130 original illustrations by Tenniel, Carroll, and others. "Addicts will be grateful . . . there is nothing for the faithful to do but sit down and fall to the banquet," N. Y. Times. Index to first lines. xiv + 446pp. 5⅜ x 8.
T654 Paperbound $1.85

DIVERSIONS AND DIGRESSIONS OF LEWIS CARROLL. A major new treasure for Carroll fans! Rare privately published humor, fantasy, puzzles, and games by Carroll at his whimsical best, with a new vein of frank satire. Includes many new mathematical amusements and recreations, among them the fragmentary Part III of "Curiosa Mathematica." Contains "The Rectory Umbrella," "The New Belfry," "The Vision of the Three T's," and much more. New 32-page supplement of rare photographs taken by Carroll. x + 375pp. 5⅜ x 8.
T732 Paperbound $1.65

THE COMPLETE NONSENSE OF EDWARD LEAR. This is the only complete edition of this master of gentle madness available at a popular price. A BOOK OF NONSENSE, NONSENSE SONGS, MORE NONSENSE SONGS AND STORIES in their entirety with all the old favorites that have delighted children and adults for years. The Dong With A Luminous Nose, The Jumblies, The Owl and the Pussycat, and hundreds of other bits of wonderful nonsense. 214 limericks, 3 sets of Nonsense Botany, 5 Nonsense Alphabets, 546 drawings by Lear himself, and much more. 320pp. 5⅜ x 8.
T167 Paperbound $1.00

THE MELANCHOLY LUTE, The Humorous Verse of Franklin P. Adams ("FPA"). The author's own selection of light verse, drawn from thirty years of FPA's column, "The Conning Tower," syndicated all over the English-speaking world. Witty, perceptive, literate, these ninety-six poems range from parodies of other poets, Millay, Longfellow, Edgar Guest, Kipling, Masefield, etc., and free and hilarious translations of Horace and other Latin poets, to satiric comments on fabled American institutions—the New York Subways, preposterous ads, suburbanites, sensational journalism, etc. They reveal with vigor and clarity the humor, integrity and restraint of a wise and gentle American satirist. Introduction by Robert Hutchinson. vi + 122pp. 5⅜ x 8½.
T108 Paperbound $1.00

SINGULAR TRAVELS, CAMPAIGNS, AND ADVENTURES OF BARON MUNCHAUSEN, R. E. Raspe, with 90 illustrations by Gustave Doré. The first edition in over 150 years to reestablish the deeds of the Prince of Liars exactly as Raspe first recorded them in 1785—the genuine Baron Munchausen, one of the most popular personalities in English literature. Included also are the best of the many sequels, written by other hands. Introduction on Raspe by J. Carswell. Bibliography of early editions. xliv + 192pp. 5⅜ x 8.
T698 Paperbound $1.00

THE WIT AND HUMOR OF OSCAR WILDE, ed. by Alvin Redman. Wilde at his most brilliant, in 1000 epigrams exposing weaknesses and hypocrisies of "civilized" society. Divided into 49 categories—sin, wealth, women, America, etc.—to aid writers, speakers. Includes excerpts from his trials, books, plays, criticism. Formerly "The Epigrams of Oscar Wilde." Introduction by Vyvyan Holland, Wilde's only living son. Introductory essay by editor. 260pp. 5⅜ x 8.
T602 Paperbound $1.00

MAX AND MORITZ, Wilhelm Busch. Busch is one of the great humorists of all time, as well as the father of the modern comic strip. This volume, translated by H. A. Klein and other hands, contains the perennial favorite "Max and Moritz" (translated by C. T. Brooks), Plisch and Plum, Das Rabennest, Eispeter, and seven other whimsical, sardonic, jovial, diabolical cartoon and verse stories. Lively English translations parallel the original German. This work has delighted millions, since it first appeared in the 19th century, and is guaranteed to please almost anyone. Edited by H. A. Klein, with an afterword. x + 205pp. 5⅝ x 8½.
T181 Paperbound $1.00

HYPOCRITICAL HELENA, Wilhelm Busch. A companion volume to "Max and Moritz," with the title piece (Die Fromme Helena) and 10 other highly amusing cartoon and verse stories, all newly translated by H. A. Klein and M. C. Klein: Adventure on New Year's Eve (Abenteuer in der Neujahrsnacht), Hangover on the Morning after New Year's Eve (Der Katzenjammer am Neujahrsmorgen), etc. English and German in parallel columns. Hours of pleasure, also a fine language aid. x + 205pp. 5⅝ x 8½.
T184 Paperbound $1.00

THE BEAR THAT WASN'T, Frank Tashlin. What does it mean? Is it simply delightful wry humor, or a charming story of a bear who wakes up in the midst of a factory, or a satire on Big Business, or an existential cartoon-story of the human condition, or a symbolization of the struggle between conformity and the individual? New York Herald Tribune said of the first edition: ". . . a fable for grownups that will be fun for children. Sit down with the book and get your own bearings." Long an underground favorite with readers of all ages and opinions. v + 51pp. Illustrated. 5⅜ x 8½.
T939 Paperbound 75¢

RUTHLESS RHYMES FOR HEARTLESS HOMES and MORE RUTHLESS RHYMES FOR HEARTLESS HOMES, Harry Graham ("Col. D. Streamer"). Two volumes of Little Willy and 48 other poetic disasters. A bright, new reprint of oft-quoted, never forgotten, devastating humor by a precursor of today's "sick" joke school. For connoisseurs of wicked, wacky humor and all who delight in the comedy of manners. Original drawings are a perfect complement. 61 illustrations. Index. vi + 69pp. Two vols. bound as one. 5⅜ x 8½.
T930 Paperbound 75¢

Teach Yourself

These British books are the most effective series of home study books on the market! With no outside help they will teach you as much as is necessary to have a good background in each subject, in many cases offering as much material as a similar high school or college course. They are carefully planned, written by foremost British educators, and amply provided with test questions and problems for you to check your progress; the mathematics books are especially rich in examples and problems. Do not confuse them with skimpy outlines or ordinary school texts or vague generalized popularizations; each book is complete in itself, full without being overdetailed, and designed to give you an easily-acquired branch of knowledge.

TEACH YOURSELF ALGEBRA, P. Abbott. The equivalent of a thorough high school course, up through logarithms. 52 illus. 307pp. 4¼ x 7.   T680 Clothbound **$2.00**

TEACH YOURSELF GEOMETRY, P. Abbott. Plane and solid geometry, covering about a year of plane and six months of solid. 268 illus. 344pp. 4½ x 7.   T681 Clothbound **$2.00**

TEACH YOURSELF TRIGONOMETRY, P. Abbott. Background of algebra and geometry will enable you to get equivalent of elementary college course. Tables. 102 illus. 204pp. 4½ x 7.   T682 Clothbound **$2.00**

TEACH YOURSELF THE CALCULUS, P. Abbott. With algebra and trigonometry you will be able to acquire a good working knowledge of elementary integral calculus and differential calculus. Excellent supplement to any course textbook. 380pp. 4¼ x 7.   T683 Clothbound **$2.00**

TEACH YOURSELF THE SLIDE RULE, B. Snodgrass. Basic principles clearly explained, with many applications in engineering, business, general figuring, will enable you to pick up very useful skill. 10 illus. 207pp. 4¼ x 7.   T684 Clothbound **$2.00**

TEACH YOURSELF MECHANICS, P. Abbott. Equivalent of part course on elementary college level, with lever, parallelogram of force, friction, laws of motion, gases, etc. Fine introduction before more advanced course. 163 illus. 271pp. 4½ x 7.   T685 Clothbound **$2.00**

TEACH YOURSELF ELECTRICITY, C. W. Wilman. Current, resistance, voltage, Ohm's law, circuits, generators, motors, transformers, etc. Non-mathematical as much as possible. 115 illus. 184pp. 4¼ x 7.   T230 Clothbound **$2.00**

TEACH YOURSELF HEAT ENGINES E. DeVille. Steam and internal combustion engines; non-mathematical introduction for student, for layman wishing background, refresher for advanced student. 76 illus. 217pp. 4¼ x 7.   T237 Clothbound **$2.00**

TEACH YOURSELF TO PLAY THE PIANO, King Palmer. Companion and supplement to lessons or self study. Handy reference, too. Nature of instrument, elementary musical theory, technique of playing, interpretation, etc. 60 illus. 144pp. 4¼ x 7.   T959 Clothbound **$2.00**

TEACH YOURSELF HERALDRY AND GENEALOGY, L. G. Pine. Modern work, avoiding romantic and overpopular misconceptions. Editor of new Burke presents detailed information and commentary down to present. Best general survey. 50 illus. glossary; 129pp. 4¼ x 7.   T962 Clothbound **$2.00**

TEACH YOURSELF HANDWRITING, John L. Dumpleton. Basic Chancery cursive style is popular and easy to learn. Many diagrams. 114 illus. 192pp. 4¼ x 7.   T960 Clothbound **$2.00**

TEACH YOURSELF CARD GAMES FOR TWO, Kenneth Konstam. Many first-rate games, including old favorites like cribbage and gin and canasta as well as new lesser-known games. Extremely interesting for cards enthusiast. 60 illus. 150pp. 4¼ x 7.   T963 Clothbound **$2.00**

TEACH YOURSELF GUIDEBOOK TO THE DRAMA, Luis Vargas. Clear, rapid survey of changing fashions and forms from Aeschylus to Tennessee Williams, in all major European traditions. Plot summaries, critical comments, etc. Equivalent of a college drama course; fine cultural background 224pp. 4¼ x 7.   T961 Clothbound **$2.00**

TEACH YOURSELF THE ORGAN, Francis Routh. Excellent compendium of background material for everyone interested in organ music, whether as listener or player. 27 musical illus. 158pp. 4¼ x 7.   T977 Clothbound **$2.00**

TEACH YOURSELF TO STUDY SCULPTURE, William Gaunt. Noted British cultural historian surveys culture from Greeks, primitive world, to moderns. Equivalent of college survey course. 23 figures, 40 photos. 158pp. 4¼ x 7.   T976 Clothbound **$2.00**

Miscellaneous

THE COMPLETE KANO JIU-JITSU (JUDO), H. I. Hancock and K. Higashi. Most comprehensive guide to judo, referred to as outstanding work by Encyclopaedia Britannica. Complete authentic Japanese system of 160 holds and throws, including the most spectacular, fully illustrated with 487 photos. Full text explains leverage, weight centers, pressure points, special tricks, etc.; shows how to protect yourself from almost any manner of attack though your attacker may have the initial advantage of strength and surprise. This authentic Kano system should not be confused with the many American imitations. xii + 500pp. 5⅜ x 8.
T639 Paperbound **$2.00**

THE MEMOIRS OF JACQUES CASANOVA. Splendid self-revelation by history's most engaging scoundrel—utterly dishonest with women and money, yet highly intelligent and observant. Here are all the famous duels, scandals, amours, banishments, thefts, treacheries, and imprisonments all over Europe: a life lived to the fullest and recounted with gusto in one of the greatest autobiographies of all time. What is more, these Memoirs are also one of the most trustworthy and valuable documents we have on the society and culture of the extravagant 18th century. Here are Voltaire, Louis XV, Catherine the Great, cardinals, castrati, pimps, and pawnbrokers—an entire glittering civilization unfolding before you with an unparalleled sense of actuality. Translated by Arthur Machen. Edited by F. A. Blossom. Introduction by Arthur Symons. Illustrated by Rockwell Kent. Total of xlviii + 2216pp. 5⅜ x 8.
T338 Vol I Paperbound **$2.00**
T339 Vol II Paperbound **$2.00**
T340 Vol III Paperbound **$2.00**
The set **$6.00**

BARNUM'S OWN STORY, P. T. Barnum. The astonishingly frank and gratifyingly well-written autobiography of the master showman and pioneer publicity man reveals the truth about his early career, his famous hoaxes (such as the Fejee Mermaid and the Woolly Horse), his amazing commercial ventures, his fling in politics, his feuds and friendships, his failures and surprising comebacks. A vast panorama of 19th century America's mores, amusements, and vitality. 66 new illustrations in this edition. xii + 500pp. 5⅜ x 8.
T764 Paperbound **$1.65**

THE STORY OF THE TITANIC AS TOLD BY ITS SURVIVORS, ed. by Jack Winocour. Most significant accounts of most overpowering naval disaster of modern times: all 4 authors were survivors. Includes 2 full-length, unabridged books: "The Loss of the S.S. Titanic," by Laurence Beesley, "The Truth about the Titanic," by Col. Archibald Gracie; 6 pertinent chapters from "Titanic and Other Ships," autobiography of only officer to survive, Second Officer Charles Lightoller; and a short, dramatic account by the Titanic's wireless operator, Harold Bride. 26 illus. 368pp. 5⅜ x 8.
T610 Paperbound **$1.50**

THE PHYSIOLOGY OF TASTE, Jean Anthelme Brillat-Savarin. Humorous, satirical, witty, and personal classic on joys of food and drink by 18th century French politician, litterateur. Treats the science of gastronomy, erotic value of truffles, Parisian restaurants, drinking contests; gives recipes for tunny omelette, pheasant, Swiss fondue, etc. Only modern translation of original French edition. Introduction. 41 illus. 346pp. 5⅝ x 8⅜.
T591 Paperbound **$1.50**

THE ART OF THE STORY-TELLER, M. L. Shedlock. This classic in the field of effective story-telling is regarded by librarians, story-tellers, and educators as the finest and most lucid book on the subject. The author considers the nature of the story, the difficulties of communicating stories to children, the artifices used in story-telling, how to obtain and maintain the effect of the story, and, of extreme importance, the elements to seek and those to avoid in selecting material. A 99-page selection of Miss Shedlock's most effective stories and an extensive bibliography of further material by Eulalie Steinmetz enhance the book's usefulness. xxi + 320pp. 5⅜ x 8.
T635 Paperbound **$1.50**

CREATIVE POWER: THE EDUCATION OF YOUTH IN THE CREATIVE ARTS, Hughes Mearns. In first printing considered revolutionary in its dynamic, progressive approach to teaching the creative arts; now accepted as one of the most effective and valuable approaches yet formulated. Based on the belief that every child has something to contribute, it provides in a stimulating manner invaluable and inspired teaching insights, to stimulate children's latent powers of creative expression in drama, poetry, music, writing, etc. Mearns's methods were developed in his famous experimental classes in creative education at the Lincoln School of Teachers College, Columbia Univ. Named one of the 20 foremost books on education in recent times by National Education Association. New enlarged revised 2nd edition. Introduction. 272pp. 5⅜ x 8.
T490 Paperbound **$1.75**

FREE AND INEXPENSIVE EDUCATIONAL AIDS, T. J. Pepe, Superintendent of Schools, Southbury, Connecticut. An up-to-date listing of over 1500 booklets, films, charts, etc. 5% costs less than 25¢; 1% costs more; 94% is yours for the asking. Use this material privately, or in schools from elementary to college, for discussion, vocational guidance, projects. 59 categories include health, trucking, textiles, language, weather, the blood, office practice, wild life, atomic energy, other important topics. Each item described according to contents, number of pages or running time, level. All material is educationally sound, and without political or company bias. 1st publication. Second, revised edition. Index. 244pp. 5⅜ x 8.
T663 Paperbound **$1.50**

CATALOGUE OF DOVER BOOKS

THE ROMANCE OF WORDS, E. Weekley. An entertaining collection of unusual word-histories that tracks down for the general reader the origins of more than 2000 common words and phrases in English (including British and American slang): discoveries often surprising, often humorous, that help trace vast chains of commerce in products and ideas. There are Arabic trade words, cowboy words, origins of family names, phonetic accidents, curious wanderings, folk-etymologies, etc. Index. xiii + 210pp. 5⅜ x 8. T710 Paperbound **$1.25**

PHRASE AND WORD ORIGINS: A STUDY OF FAMILIAR EXPRESSIONS, A. H. Holt. One of the most entertaining books on the unexpected origins and colorful histories of words and phrases, based on sound scholarship, but written primarily for the layman. Over 1200 phrases and 1000 separate words are covered, with many quotations, and the results of the most modern linguistic and historical researches. "A right jolly book Mr. Holt has made," N. Y. Times. v + 254pp. 5⅜ x 8. T758 Paperbound **$1.35**

AMATEUR WINE MAKING, S. M. Tritton. Now, with only modest equipment and no prior knowledge, you can make your own fine table wines. A practical handbook, this covers every type of grape wine, as well as fruit, flower, herb, vegetable, and cereal wines, and many kinds of mead, cider, and beer. Every question you might have is answered, and there is a valuable discussion of what can go wrong at various stages along the way. Special supplement of yeasts and American sources of supply. 13 tables. 32 illustrations. Glossary. Index. 239pp. 5½ x 8½. T514 Clothbound **$4.00**

SAILING ALONE AROUND THE WORLD. Captain Joshua Slocum. A great modern classic in a convenient inexpensive edition. Captain Slocum's account of his single-handed voyage around the world in a 34 foot boat which he rebuilt himself. A nearly unparalleled feat of seamanship told with vigor, wit, imagination, and great descriptive power. "A nautical equivalent of Thoreau's account," Van Wyck Brooks. 67 illustrations. 308pp. 5⅜ x 8. T326 Paperbound **$1.00**

FARES, PLEASE! by J. A. Miller. Authoritative, comprehensive, and entertaining history of local public transit from its inception to its most recent developments: trolleys, horsecars, streetcars, buses, elevateds, subways, along with monorails, "road-railers," and a host of other extraordinary vehicles. Here are all the flamboyant personalities involved, the vehement arguments, the unusual information, and all the nostalgia. "Interesting facts brought into especially vivid life," N. Y. Times. New preface. 152 illustrations, 4 new. Bibliography. xix + 204pp. 5⅜ x 8. T671 Paperbound **$1.50**

HOAXES, C. D. MacDougall. Shows how art, science, history, journalism can be perverted for private purposes. Hours of delightful entertainment and a work of scholarly value, this often shocking book tells of the deliberate creation of nonsense news, the Cardiff giant, Shakespeare forgeries, the Loch Ness monster, Biblical frauds, political schemes, literary hoaxers like Chatterton, Ossian, the disumbrationist school of painting, the lady in black at Valentino's tomb, and over 250 others. It will probably reveal the truth about a few things you've believed, and help you spot more readily the editorial "gander" and planted publicity release. "A stupendous collection . . . and shrewd analysis." New Yorker. New revised edition. 54 photographs. Index. 320pp. 5⅜ x 8. T465 Paperbound **$1.75**

A HISTORY OF THE WARFARE OF SCIENCE WITH THEOLOGY IN CHRISTENDOM, A. D. White. Most thorough account ever written of the great religious-scientific battles shows gradual victory of science over ignorant, harmful beliefs. Attacks on theory of evolution; attacks on Galileo; great medieval plagues caused by belief in devil-origin of disease; attacks on Franklin's experiments with electricity; the witches of Salem; scores more that will amaze you. Author, co-founder and first president of Cornell U., writes with vast scholarly background, but in clear, readable prose. Acclaimed as classic effort in America to do away with superstition. Index. Total of 928pp. 5⅜ x 8. T608 Vol I Paperbound **$1.85**
T609 Vol II Paperbound **$1.85**

THE SHIP OF FOOLS, Sebastian Brant. First printed in 1494 in Basel, this amusing book swept Europe, was translated into almost every important language, and was a best-seller for centuries. That it is still living and vital is shown by recent developments in publishing. This is the only English translation of this work, and it recaptures in lively, modern verse all the wit and insights of the original, in satirizations of foibles and vices: greed, adultery, envy, hatred, sloth, profiteering, etc. This will long remain the definitive English edition, for Professor Zeydel has provided biography of Brant, bibliography, publishing history, influences, etc. Complete reprint of 1944 edition. Translated by Professor E. Zeydel, University of Cincinnati. All 114 original woodcut illustrations. viii + 399pp. 5½ x 8⅝. T266 Paperbound **$2.00**

ERASMUS, A STUDY OF HIS LIFE, IDEALS AND PLACE IN HISTORY, Preserved Smith. This is the standard English biography and evaluation of the great Netherlands humanist Desiderius Erasmus. Written by one of the foremost American historians it covers all aspects of Erasmus's life, his influence in the religious quarrels of the Reformation, his overwhelming role in the field of letters, and his importance in the emergence of the new world view of the Northern Renaissance. This is not only a work of great scholarship, it is also an extremely interesting, vital portrait of a great man. 8 illustrations. xiv + 479pp. 5⅝ x 8½. T331 Paperbound **$2.00**

New Books

101 PATCHWORK PATTERNS, Ruby Short McKim. With no more ability than the fundamentals of ordinary sewing, you will learn to make over 100 beautiful quilts: flowers, rainbows, Irish chains, fish and bird designs, leaf designs, unusual geometric patterns, many others. Cutting designs carefully diagrammed and described, suggestions for materials, yardage estimates, step-by-step instructions, plus entertaining stories of origins of quilt names, other folklore. Revised 1962. 101 full-sized patterns. 140 illustrations. Index. 128pp. 7⅞ x 10¾.
T773 Paperbound **$1.85**

ESSENTIAL GRAMMAR SERIES
By concentrating on the essential core of material that constitutes the semantically most important forms and areas of a language and by stressing explanation (often bringing parallel English forms into the discussion) rather than rote memory, this new series of grammar books is among the handiest language aids ever devised. Designed by linguists and teachers for adults with limited learning objectives and learning time, these books omit nothing important, yet they teach more usable language material and do it more quickly and permanently than any other self-study material. Clear and rigidly economical, they concentrate upon immediately usable language material, logically organized so that related material is always presented together. Any reader of typical capability can use them to refresh his grasp of language, to supplement self-study language records or conventional grammars used in schools, or to begin language study on his own. Now available:

ESSENTIAL GERMAN GRAMMAR, Dr. Guy Stern & E. F. Bleiler. Index. Glossary of terms. 128pp. 5⅜ x 8.
T422 Paperbound **$1.00**

ESSENTIAL FRENCH GRAMMAR, Dr. Seymour Resnick. Index. Cognate list. Glossary. 159pp. 5⅜ x 8.
T419 Paperbound **$1.00**

ESSENTIAL ITALIAN GRAMMAR, Dr. Olga Ragusa. Index. Glossary. 111pp. 5⅜ x 8.
T779 Paperbound **$1.00**

ESSENTIAL SPANISH GRAMMAR, Dr. Seymour Resnick. Index. 50-page cognate list. Glossary. 138pp. 5⅜ x 8.
T780 Paperbound **$1.00**

PHILOSOPHIES OF MUSIC HISTORY: A Study of General Histories of Music, 1600-1960, Warren D. Allen. Unquestionably one of the most significant documents yet to appear in musicology, this thorough survey covers the entire field of historical research in music. An influential masterpiece of scholarship, it includes early music histories; theories on the ethos of music; lexicons, dictionaries and encyclopedias of music; musical historiography through the centuries; philosophies of music history; scores of related topics. Copiously documented. New preface brings work up to 1960. Index. 317-item bibliography. 9 illustrations; 3 full-page plates. 5⅜ x 8½. xxxiv + 382pp.
T282 Paperbound **$2.00**

MR. DOOLEY ON IVRYTHING AND IVRYBODY, Finley Peter Dunne. The largest collection in print of hilarious utterances by the irrepressible Irishman of Archey Street, one of the most vital characters in American fiction. Gathered from the half dozen books that appeared during the height of Mr. Dooley's popularity, these 102 pieces are all unaltered and uncut, and they are all remarkably fresh and pertinent even today. Selected and edited by Robert Hutchinson. 5⅜ x 8½. xii + 244p.
T626 Paperbound **$1.00**

TREATISE ON PHYSIOLOGICAL OPTICS, Hermann von Helmholtz. Despite new investigations, this important work will probably remain preeminent. Contains everything known about physiological optics up to 1925, covering scores of topics under the general headings of dioptrics of the eye, sensations of vision, and perecptions of vision. Von Helmholtz's voluminous data are all included, as are extensive supplementary matter incorporated into the third German edition, new material prepared for 1925 English edition, and copious textual annotations by J. P. C. Southall. The most exhaustive treatise ever prepared on the subject, it has behind it a list of contributors that will never again be duplicated. Translated and edited by J. P. C. Southall. Bibliography. Indexes. 312 illustrations. 3 volumes bound as 2. Total of 1749pp. 5⅜ x 8.
S15-16 Two volume set, Clothbound **$15.00**

THE ARTISTIC ANATOMY OF TREES, Rex Vicat Cole. Even the novice with but an elementary knowledge of drawing and none of the structure of trees can learn to draw, paint trees from this systematic, lucid instruction book. Copiously illustrated with the author's own sketches, diagrams, and 50 paintings from the early Renaissance to today, it covers composition; structure of twigs, boughs, buds, branch systems; outline forms of major species; how leaf is set on twig; flowers and fruit and their arrangement; etc. 500 illustrations. Bibliography. Indexes. 347pp. 5⅜ x 8.
T1016 Clothbound **$4.50**

CATALOGUE OF DOVER BOOKS

CHANCE, LUCK AND STATISTICS, H. C. Levinson. The theory of chance, or probability, and the science of statistics presented in simple, non-technical language. Covers fundamentals by analyzing games of chance, then applies those fundamentals to immigration and birth rates, operations research, stock speculation, insurance rates, advertising, and other fields. Excellent course supplement and a delightful introduction for non-mathematicians. Formerly "The Science of Chance." Index. xiv + 356pp. 5⅜ x 8.   T1007 Paperbound **$1.85**

THROUGH THE ALIMENTARY CANAL WITH GUN AND CAMERA: A Fascinating Trip to the Interior, George S. Chappell. An intrepid explorer, better known as a major American humorist, accompanied by imaginary camera-man and botanist, conducts this unforgettably hilarious journey to the human interior. Wildly imaginative, his account satirizes academic pomposity, parodies cliché-ridden travel literature, and cleverly uses facts of physiology for comic purposes. All the original line drawings by Otto Soglow are included to add to the merriment. Preface by Robert Benchley. 17 illustrations. xii + 116pp. 5⅜ x 8½.   T376 Paperbound **$1.00**

TALKS TO TEACHERS ON PSYCHOLOGY and to Students on Some of Life's Ideals, William James. America's greatest psychologist invests these lectures with immense personal charm, invaluable insights, and superb literary style. 15 Harvard lectures, 3 lectures delivered to students in New England touch upon psychology and the teaching of art, stream of consciousness, the child as a behaving organism, education and behavior, association of ideas, the gospel of relaxation, what makes life significant, and other related topics. Interesting, and still vital pedagogy. x + 146pp. 5⅜ x 8½.   T261 Paperbound **$1.00**

A WHIMSEY ANTHOLOGY, collected by Carolyn Wells. Delightful verse on the lighter side: logical whimsies, poems shaped like decanters and flagons, lipograms and acrostics, alliterative verse, enigmas and charades, anagrams, linguistic and dialectic verse, tongue twisters, limericks, travesties, and just about very other kind of whimsical poetry ever written. Works by Edward Lear, Gelett Burgess, Poe, Lewis Carroll, Henley, Robert Herrick, Christina Rossetti, scores of other poets will entertain and amuse you for hours. Index. xiv + 221pp. 5⅜ x 8½.
T1020 Paperbound **$1.25**

LANDSCAPE PAINTING, R. O. Dunlop. A distinguished modern artist is a perfect guide to the aspiring landscape painter. This practical book imparts to even the uninitiated valuable methods and techniques. Useful advice is interwoven throughout a fascinating illustrated history of landscape painting, from Ma Yüan to Picasso. 60 half-tone reproductions of works by Giotto, Giovanni Bellini, Piero della Francesca, Tintoretto, Giorgione, Raphael, Van Ruisdael, Poussin, Gainsborough, Monet, Cezanne, Seurat, Picasso, many others. Total of 71 illustrations, 4 in color. Index. 192pp. 7⅜ x 10.   T1018 Clothbound **$6.00**

PRACTICAL LANDSCAPE PAINTING, Adrian Stokes. A complete course in landscape painting that trains the senses to perceive as well as the hand to apply the principles underlying the pictorial aspect of nature. Author fully explains tools, value and nature of various colors, and instructs beginners in clear, simple terms how to apply them. Places strong emphasis on drawing and composition, foundations often neglected in painting texts. Includes pictorial-textual survey of the art from Ancient China to the present, with helpful critical comments and numerous diagrams illustrating every stage. 93 illustrations. Index. 256pp. 5⅜ x 8.
T1017 Clothbound **$3.75**

PELLUCIDAR, THREE NOVELS: AT THE EARTH'S CORE, PELLUCIDAR, TANAR OF PELLUCIDAR, Edgar Rice Burroughs. The first three novels of adventure in the thrill-filled world within the hollow interior of the earth. David Innes's mechanical mole drills through the outer crust and precipitates him into an astonishing world. Among Burroughs's most popular work. Illustrations by J. Allan St. John. 5⅜ x 8½.   T1051 Paperbound **$2.00**
T1050 Clothbound **$3.75**

JOE MILLER'S JESTS OR, THE WITS VADE-MECUM. Facsimile of the first edition of famous 18th century collection of repartees, bons mots, puns and jokes, the father of the humor anthology. A first-hand look at the taste of fashionable London in the Age of Pope. 247 entertaining anecdotes, many involving well-known personages such as Colley Cibber, Sir Thomas More, Rabelais, rich in humor, historic interest. New introduction contains biographical information on Joe Miller, fascinating history of his enduring collection, bibliographical information on collections of comic material. Introduction by Robert Hutchinson. 96pp. 5⅜ x 8½.
Paperbound **$1.00**

THE HUMOROUS WORLD OF JEROME K. JEROME. Complete essays and extensive passages from nine out-of-print books ("Three Men on Wheels," "Novel Notes," "Told After Supper," "Sketches in Lavender, Blue and Green," "American Wives and Others," 4 more) by a highly original humorist, author of the novel "Three Men in a Boat." Human nature is JKJ's subject: the problems of husbands, of wives, of tourists, of the human animal trapped in the drawing room. His sympathetic acceptance of the shortcomings of his race and his ability to see humor in almost any situation make this a treasure for those who know his work and a pleasant surprise for those who don't. Edited and with an introduction by Robert Hutchinson. xii + 260pp. 5⅜ x 8½.   T58 Paperbound **$1.00**

CATALOGUE OF DOVER BOOKS

GEOMETRY OF FOUR DIMENSIONS, H. P. Manning. Unique in English as a clear, concise intro-
duction to this fascinating subject. Treatment is primarily synthetic and Euclidean, although
hyperplanes and hyperspheres at infinity are considered by non-Euclidean forms. Historical
introduction and foundations of 4-dimensional geometry; perpendicularity; simple angles;
angles of planes; higher order; symmetry; order, motion; hyperpyramids, hypercones, hyper-
spheres; figures with parallel elements; volume, hypervolume in space; regular polyhedroids.
Glossary of terms. 74 illustrations. ix + 348pp. 5⅜ x 8. S182 Paperbound **$2.00**

PAPER FOLDING FOR BEGINNERS, W. D. Murray and F. J. Rigney. A delightful introduction to
the varied and entertaining Japanese art of origami (paper folding), with a full, crystal-clear
text that anticipates every difficulty; over 275 clearly labeled diagrams of all important stages
in creation. You get results at each stage, since complex figures are logically developed from
simpler ones. 43 different pieces are explained: sailboats, frogs, roosters, etc. 6 photographic
plates. 279 diagrams. 95pp. 5⅝ x 8⅜. T713 Paperbound **$1.00**

SATELLITES AND SCIENTIFIC RESEARCH, D. King-Hele. An up-to-the-minute non-technical ac-
count of the man-made satellites and the discoveries they have yielded up to September of
1961. Brings together information hitherto published only in hard-to-get scientific journals. In-
cludes the life history of a typical satellite, methods of tracking, new information on the
shape of the earth, zones of radiation, etc. Over 60 diagrams and 6 photographs. Mathemati-
cal appendix. Bibliography of over 100 items. Index. xii + 180pp. 5⅜ x 8½.
T703 Paperbound **$2.00**

LOUIS PASTEUR, S. J. Holmes. A brief, very clear, and warmly understanding biography of the
great French scientist by a former Professor of Zoology in the University of California. Traces
his home life, the fortunate effects of his education, his early researches and first theses, and
his constant struggle with superstition and institutionalism in his work on microorganisms,
fermentation, anthrax, rabies, etc. New preface by the author. 159pp. 5⅜ x 8.
T197 Paperbound **$1.00**

THE ENJOYMENT OF CHESS PROBLEMS, K. S. Howard. A classic treatise on this minor art by
an internationally recognized authority that gives a basic knowledge of terms and themes for
the everyday chess player as well as the problem fan: 7 chapters on the two-mover; 7 more
on 3- and 4-move problems; a chapter on selfmates; and much more. "The most important
one-volume contribution originating solely in the U.S.A.," Alain White. 200 diagrams. Index.
Solutions, viii + 212pp. 5⅜ x 8. T742 Paperbound **$1.25**

SAM LOYD AND HIS CHESS PROBLEMS, Alain C. White. Loyd was (for all practical purposes)
the father of the American chess problem and his protégé and successor presents here the
diamonds of his production, chess problems embodying a whimsy and bizarre fancy entirely
unique. More than 725 in all, ranging from two-mover to extremely elaborate five-movers,
including Loyd's contributions to chess oddities—problems in which pieces are arranged to
form initials, figures, other by-paths of chess problem found nowhere else. Classified accord-
ing to major concept, with full text analyzing problems, containing selections from Loyd's
own writings. A classic to challenge your ingenuity, increase your skill. Corrected republica-
tion of 1913 edition. Over 750 diagrams and illustrations. 744 problems with solutions.
471pp. 5⅜ x 8½. T928 Paperbound **$2.25**

FABLES IN SLANG & MORE FABLES IN SLANG, George Ade. 2 complete books of major
American humorist in pungent colloquial tradition of Twain, Billings. 1st reprinting in over
30 years includes "The Two Mandolin Players and the Willing Performer," "The Base Ball
Fan Who Took the Only Known Cure," "The Slim Girl Who Tried to Keep a Date that was
Never Made," 42 other tales of eccentric, perverse, but always funny characters. "Touch
of genius," H. L. Mencken. New introduction by E. F. Bleiler. 86 illus. 208pp. 5⅜ x 8.
T533 Paperbound **$1.00**